WHAT DO YOU THINK OF JESUS?

David P. Scaer

Reproduced by special permission of

David P. Scaer

Library of Congress Catalog Number 72-97341
ISBN# 0-570-03153-2
Copyright © 1999
Concordia Theological Seminary Press
Fort Wayne, Indiana
Printed by Sheridan Books, Inc.
Chelsea. Michigan 48118

Manufactured in the United States of America

What Do You Think of Jesus?

Rev. Dr. David P. Scaer

CONCORDIA
THEOLOGICAL
SEMINARY
P R E S S

TO

MY MOTHER
VICTORIA ZIMMERMANN SCAER
For many years a faithful co-worker in the Gospel
with my sainted pastor father
among the dear members
of
Trinity Evangelical Lutheran Church of Flatbush
Brooklyn, New York

CONTENTS

Chapter I. What Do You Think of Jesus?   7

Chapter II. Introducing Jesus   21

Chapter III. Jesus Versus Satan: Who Will Win?   28

Chapter IV. Jesus and the Wrath of God   36

Chapter V. King Jesus   64

Chapter VI. The King and His Kingdom   76

Chapter VII. The Son of Man: Another Strange Title   85

Chapter VIII. A Few Prophetic Allusions   90

Chapter IX. Resurrection: The Finale   104

CHAPTER I

What Do You Think of Jesus?

The Need for the Question:

Almost right in the middle of Matthew's Gospel, the evangelist records a critical episode between Jesus and His disciples. He had asked them for a sampling of current public opinion on who He really was. All of the answers indicated that Jesus was an extraordinary man. This Jewish rabbi from Nazareth brought to the minds of His listeners images of John the Baptist, whose bones were still fresh in his grave; Elijah, God's valiant warrior, who was triumphantly carried into heaven; and Jeremiah, the last bulwark in a crumbling kingdom. Or could it be that Jesus was another prophet or a new one appearing on the scene? But none of these opinions are satisfactory, simply because Jesus is above the categories they suggest.

Jesus is simply not one among many. He is more than just a historically great person. He was not a great writer like Shakespeare or Plato. In fact there are no books which He left behind. There are no monuments like the aqueducts or the Colosseum recalling His accomplishments. The political and cultural history of the first century A. D. could very well be written without His name. Born in Palestine, He never left the immediate surroundings. As He was virtually unknown outside His own country, the contemporary writers of antiquity make no mention of Him until at least two generations after His death. Even then the reference is more to His followers rather than to Him. Still the teacher from Nazareth, that insignificant town which had a reputation for producing inconsequential persons, asks the question of His followers, "But who do you think I am?" By what right does anyone dare to ask this kind of question? Jesus doesn't ask,

"What am I doing?" or even "What do people think I am doing?" Jesus' question suggests that He must *be* something other people are not. In spite of varied public opinions concerning His work, all attest that Jesus is some kind of special man through whom God is working.

Some people have thought that Jesus was having a crisis with both His identity and His task and was asking for some assistance in determining who He really was and what He was really doing. Obviously He was Jesus from Nazareth, who was currently engaged in preaching. But the question deserves a more profound answer. Jesus is not looking for information about Himself, but commitment which is beneath the superficial from others concerning Himself.

With this question, "But who do you think I am?" Jesus places Himself before Peter, the disciples, and every man who comes into the world and demands from him a decision on which he is willing to stake his total existence, even to the point of death. The question is addressed to each man and no one can answer for another. How other people have answered the question is interesting and informative, but it does not remove the burden of a demanded answer. Refusing to answer the question or pretending the question does not exist is in itself an answer — negative! But simple confrontation with the question is not enough, because not every answer is acceptable.

Jesus brushes aside the suggestions that He is only a prophet or a unique instrument for God's will among men. He pushes Peter and every man who belongs to Him to the only acceptable conclusion: He is the Christ, God's Son. This is the ultimate answer and reality — and thus also the final truth. It is revealed by God and surpasses the ordinary dimensions of human knowledge. Nothing can surpass this. This confession becomes verdict, and every man will have to stand under it and be judged by God. Our task is to answer the question of what it means to be Christ, God's Son.

Did Jesus Really Live?

In a survey made in Great Britain in 1970, the question was

posed to people concerning whom they considered their most admired person. Jesus Christ was the first choice, though Winston Churchill was a close runner-up. The question of whether Jesus really lived is not a problem for most people, even for those who are unchurched and have no commitment to the religion that bears His name by being called *Christian.*

The name of Jesus Christ is well entrenched in many cultures of the world, and sayings traditionally attributed to Him are commonly used. Abraham Lincoln's speech on "House Divided" reapplies the words of Jesus concerning Satan's kingdom that a house divided against itself cannot stand. The Sermon on the Mount can provide slogans for any humane cause and has at times been used even by communists, who are unalterably opposed to Christianity and committed to its extermination. The near universal celebration of Christmas, even in a country like Japan, which has no Christian culture, recalls the birth of Jesus. If contemporary indications were by themselves sufficient evidence, then we would have to conclude that there must have been a Jesus. Almost 20 centuries of Western culture would yield the same kind of results.

Still one segment of New Testament scholarship seriously doubts whether Jesus really ever existed; and the most prominent scholars in the field have concluded that even if Jesus did exist as a real person, we can have no certain knowledge of who He was and what He did. Rudolph Bultmann, who is the most famous of these scholars, asserts with as much certainty as is possible for him only that Jesus died under Pontius Pilate and that the rest of the data contained in the Gospels is the religious and pious reflection of His followers.

Some of his students are a little more venturesome and see several passages in the Gospels as having actually originated with Jesus, though their context in the Gospels may be quite different from the original intent of Jesus. The more radical theologians see no historical connection between what we have in the Gospels and the real person of Jesus Himself.

This type of thinking is influenced by a philosophy called existentialism. It teaches that all truth is in the present or future, and it is both impossible and useless to recover any figure from the past, including Jesus. The prime concern for this kind of "Christianity" is "What Jesus means to me?" with all the weight of this put on the words *"to me."* The search for a real Jesus might safely be relegated to a position of unimportance for a Christian who confesses in both his words and actions the name of Jesus, but for the fact that for nearly two centuries scholars of considerable influence and prominence have sincerely doubted whether the Gospel records of Jesus are really accurate in any sense at all. Their ideas have filtered down from the seminaries into the pulpit and from there into the pews. There is a general consensus that there might have been a Jesus, but that the miraculous things attributed to Him were the pious inventions of His disciples. Some scholars have gone one step further and have claimed that the New Testament is essentially the religious reflections of early Christian congregations in the last half of the first century A. D., and not those of the apostles.

Regardless of how unpleasant the task is of answering the questions of whether or not Jesus lived and did the things and said the sayings attributed to Him by the evangelists, these questions must be answered, if for no other reason, than for ordinary honesty. Should we conclude that Jesus did not live or that His reality is shrouded in the mist of an unclear past, then there is little reason for holding Him up to all people as a crucial factor in their lives and as one who demands commitment to Himself.

The Christian church must at least meet the minimum standards of other groups which have been formed to honor the person and teachings of other men. What would be the appeal of a Lincoln society if historical scholars concluded that Abraham Lincoln did not work for the freeing of the slaves and the unification of the nation, but that all this was the fabrication of some sincere American patroit? The example is not so far fetched.

Recently, in the state of Illinois, a prominent state elected official died with a hoard of nearly a million dollars stashed away in shoe boxes. The origin of this money has not yet been accounted for. A civic-minded organization has had to wrestle with the problem of whether a young peoples citizenship award, named to honor this man, should be made before the matter is cleared up. To date nothing has been conclusively proved, but doubts concerning his honesty and political integrity have caused hesitation in the minds of even the most politically uncommitted people.

The Christian church is more than a goverment, a political party, or a patriotic society, but she must at least meet the same standards of integrity, if not higher ones. She still presents herself as the bastion of morality and in some cases has appointed herself as the political conscience of the nation. By what right is the church exempt from scrutiny, especially as it concerns the center of her attention, Jesus Christ, and her founders, the disciples? If we are not willing to ask the questions of historical authenticity of the Gospels, then the church has no right to credibility. How can she ask honesty of others if she exempts herself? Unless we can affirm without doubt that Jesus lived, can we pose His question of what people think of Him? The words "I am" must be affirmed before we can pose Jesus' question, "But who do you think that *I am*?"

How Close Can We Get to the Person of "Jesus"

The question of whether or not Jesus really lived must be preceded by the question of how close can we get to Jesus. The man of faith will immediately respond that since Jesus is alive in him through faith He is as close as his own heart. He feels no need for any historical journeys into the past since Jesus is a living reality for him. This would suffice if Christianity were only a philosophy which gave man a certain perspective to life. This would suffice if Christianity were like a Greek myth that took place somewhere out there beyond the clouds and the skies or in the imagination of the mind. But the message of Christianity is that *Someone* actually lived *somewhere* at *some time*. Not *any*one at *any* place at *any* time. Christianity's message claims that it can be tied down historically, chronologically, and geographically.

The winds of time have swept many things away, but still tourists flock to Palestine since many of the places mentioned in the Gospels are still extant. Of course the land is dotted with pious

11

forgeries — frequently erected for the delight of the tourists and the financial benefit of the inhabitants. Nevertheless, many of the steps of Jesus as recorded in the Gospels can be retraced.

Christianity proclaims for faith a message, a message about a happening in time, our time. No one can totally recover the past or relive it, but the past can be blocked out by calendars and maps. In this, Jesus is no different from any other figure from the past. The broad outlines and boundaries of His life can be sketched on the map of Palestine during the reigns of the Roman emperors Caesar Augustus and his stepson, Tiberius Caesar. Each time the church confesses the Apostles and Nicene Creed she anchors her faith to time and place with the words "under Pontius Pilate."

By the year 100 A. D. there were outcroppings of Jesus talk in all corners of the Roman Empire. Something must have happened during the preceding century, as no one was talking about Jesus of Nazareth in the year 1 A. D. Groups of people called churches were springing up like weeds. The members of these churches were not united by the things that ordinarily bring people together. They had different economic and political interests. Some were slaveholders, some free men, and others slaves. All types of occupations were represented in these groups. Soldiers, women of the street, merchants, and people close to the emperor himself could be found in their gatherings. Their common interest could not be explained by race, culture or language — all of which are ordinarily basic for the cohesiveness of a community. The churches reflected in their members the wide diversion of the Roman Empire itself. Their unity could not merely be explained sociologically. This is not to say that they had perfect harmony and that no problems existed; however, all of them were focusing their attention on a certain "Jesus" who had been put to death in the city of Jerusalem and came back to life.

From the third decade of the first century, Christianity had spread very rapidly, so that in two generations it had reached the imperial household in Rome. Pliny the Younger wrote a letter to Emperor Trajan in Rome in 110 A. D. on how to handle Christians whom he considered a blight on the Roman Empire. Tacitus gives a report of the burning of Rome in 64 A. D., where the followers of "Chrestus" were blamed for this incendiary action. We as Christians do not feel compelled to answer this historical charge of arson, but we do know that in hardly more than a generation after Jesus there were people called "Christians" in honor of a certain "Christ, who was condemned to death during the reign of Tiberius by the procurator Pontius Pilate."

The date A. D. 64 is significant for the world to be taking note of the young movement, as the movement itself was still in the process of growing. Many, perhaps most, of the apostles were still alive. Some of the books in our New Testament were still to be written. The church was still on the launching pad but had already become a political factor in Rome, the center of the world.

For every event in the world there is a historical cause. Frequently there are many causes and it is difficult to single out the most prominent ones. Determining historical causes is a complex job. For example, the financial depression of the late 1920s and early '30s was at least one cause, if not the most important one, in the election of Franklin Roosevelt as president of the United States in 1932.

Christianity had become a historical phenomenon. There must have been at *least* one cause for it. Before A. D. 70 it was already recognized as some kind of religion whose followers might have political designs. Subsequent persecution of these churches in the next three centuries, frequently on political grounds, was only a continuance of this assumption, even though it was a false assumption. Who or what started it?

For example, Mohammedanism can be traced right back to the sixth-century prophet whose religion often bears his name. Why did Christianity all of a sudden pop up? There was really no need for a new religion in the empire. Jews were not that plentiful at that time, but they offered a strict monotheism for those so inclined. The Romans and Greeks had a pantheon of gods which could fit the whims, desires, fancies, and needs of most anyone. Worship of the emperor was common everywhere. For the more rustic and less cultured individual there were the gods of the barbarian tribes to the north that were already stirring up trouble for

13

the empire. For the mystics there were the mystery rites of the east with the cult of Mithra. Those who were opposed to gods could always opt for an atheistic philosophy that both denied the existence of the gods and made sport of their foolish antics as they chased each other around the heavens. Why the need for Christianity?

There was no lack of religious diversity in the first-century world. Religious tastes of every type never went hungry. Explaining the origin of Christianity as a religious invention to fill a deep-seated psychological need is totally unsatisfactory. Besides, religious inventions and myths grow up over many years, even centuries. But there was no great period of time between the life of Jesus and the time when a full-blown religion dedicated to Him had become a recognized reality in the empire — it took not even two generations. There simply is not enough evidence to explain Christianity as a religious fabrication.

As Confucius is responsible for the philosophy that bears his name and Mohammed originated his religion, so the best historical probability is that Jesus really lived and is responsible for the teachings of Christianity. In fact the variety of written records for Jesus is much greater than those for Caesar Augustus, the Roman emperor at the time of Jesus' birth and boyhood. This evidence for establishing the historical probability for a real Jesus is not offered by faith or for faith. It is used only to show that apart from the church's faith, the evidence for establishing Jesus' existence is as good as, if not better than, any of His contemporaries.

Finding Jesus in the Gospels

As we have seen, non-Christian sources take us within less than 40 years of Jesus' life. In addition there are Christian sources called "Gospels" which come from the first century. It is debatable how many of them were written before or after A. D. 64, but all of them claim to have intimate and authentic knowledge of what Jesus said and did. Some claim first-hand acquaintance with Him. Up to this point the historical arguments from the organization of a universal church dedicated to Jesus and the mention of His

14

name in a couple of non-Christian sources have only been used to demonstrate that the evidence points to the existence of a Palestinian Jew, known as "Jesus." The Gospels assume His existence and fill in not a few details about His message, His actions, His dealing with friends and enemies, and a few essential biographical details about His conception, birth, death, and resurrection. This is not saying that we have a complete biography, but there is enough information about Jesus that we can easily come to certain conclusions about Him. The impossibility of even a near total reconstruction of His life is no excuse for historical agnosticism.

Some scholars within and without the church have questioned the historical reliability of the Gospels by claiming that these documents are biased writings produced by His followers and that the marks of historical objectivity are lacking. The Gospels are not written, so they claim, as history books should be written. (How *should* history books be written?) The church does not hide from the charge that the Gospels were written by the friends and followers of Jesus and in His favor; but this alone is hardly sufficient evidence to count them as being inaccurate concerning the events they relate.

Frequently it is stated that the Gospels do not present the same type of photographic report that a modern newspaper or TV telecast presents. I think that a compliment! The credibility gap in news reporting and official government releases is a source of concern for many people.

In all newspapers the editorials begin with the headlines and main news stories and not with the section explicitly marked "Editorials." All writing, with maybe an exception like the telephone directory, is subjective and prejudicial. Even dictionaries approach only an agreed upon objectivity. Everyone sees events and interprets them through his own eyes.

The question of who was really responsible for the Chicago riots of 1968 in connection with the Democratic national convention will never, at least in our generation, be answered to the satisfaction of even all the eyewitnesses. Not even television has rescued us from subjectivity. If anything, it is a very unobjective medium of communication. Evaluations of the Chicago riots by the next generations will hardly be more satisfactory since they will be living in another milieu and will not have been at the scene. The criticisms leveled against the Gospels as being a subjective and biased revealing of the sentiments of the writers can be leveled against any type of reporting and writing—even the society page in a newspaper.

In comparison with other writings from the same period the Gospels demonstrate an uncanny and sometimes uncomfortable sobriety. Julius Caesar's *Gallic Wars* always puts the author in the best possible light and varies little from the political writing that most intelligent voters take with a grain of salt today. Josephus' *Jewish War* was highly complimentary of the Emperors Vespasian and Titus; it should also contain at its conclusion the statement, "This political announcement has been paid for by . . . ." The Gospels are written—and this is not denying that they are "propaganda" literature—with an almost matter-of-fact attitude. The resurrection of Jesus is written with no more embellishment than His death. Later generations of Christians would not always exercise the same restraint.

Flowery lives of Jesus, known technically as apocryphal Gospels, falsely attributed to Thomas, Peter, and others, are so fantastic as to be downright laughable. They have rightly deserved the scant attention which only the most specialized scholars have given them. These writings are rejected out of hand.

The past can never be totally reclaimed. It cannot be rerun like a film through a motion picture projector. Even if it could, the film would not show the *whole* story. There is no way of recovering what has already happened. Who really knows the minds of those who participated in the events? Are the so-called Pentagon Papers really objective? In archeology our hands can touch and feel concrete objects, but in so many cases we have to apply interpretation to the artifacts. Centuries from now our descendants might conclude from the shapes of the openers on soft drink and beer cans that these were some type of erotic symbols. The scientific method of testing things simply does not apply to the past.

How then do we know the past? The past can never be made any closer than the documents that report it. Man is not omnipresent — even with the advent of television reporting. All knowledge about things which he does not immediately perceive is gained through reports. The Gospels are reports and should be given at least the same credibility that is given to any other report, ancient or modern. Scholars discredit them frequently because they report such miraculous events like the resurrection of Jesus. Since they have never experienced a resurrection, they conclude a priori, without any evidence, that the report of Jesus' resurrection cannot be reliable. This type of procedure is only subordinating the report to one's own preconceived notions. This is subjectivism in the extreme. If such a rule were applied in all cases, then only what already parallels my knowledge and experience could ever be possibly true. Drawn to logical conclusions, there could be no new knowledge or information.

What are the Gospels?

A favorite way of recording the past is by chronicle. Sometimes chronicles are written right on the spot. The heads of states often hire writers to write down the details of their accomplishments. President Johnson made sure that photographers captured both the official and unofficial moments of his administration for posterity. Other chronicles are written years after the events have occurred. There are other styles of writing in recording the past. Frequently the major events and important speeches of an influential person are singled out and commented on. The Gospels are written in this way.

The evangelists have taken what they consider to be the most important events in the life of Jesus and His most significant words and arranged them to attain a certain purpose. They cannot be understood unless the writers' purposes are clearly understood. Each evangelist has a slightly *different emphasis* of purpose, but each has the *same purpose*. The purpose of each Gospel is to convince the reader that Jesus is the answer to man's dilemma and predicament and that Jesus is worthy of the reader's faith and confidence. The Gospels are not chronicles in that there is an account by account record of everything which Jesus did or said. Anyway this type of literature is hardly very interesting. This does not mean that the question of chronology is in all recorded episodes unimportant. There is a definite progression in certain events of Jesus' life. Obviously His birth and death precede His resurrection. Other examples could easily be offered to demonstrate this, but chronological order is not the overarching concern. For example, from Mark's Gospel it is very difficult to determine how many years Jesus exercised His ministry. In John's Gospel there seems to have been at least three years.

The purpose of each Gospel can be generally summarized in the answer to the question which Jesus poses before His disciples, "But who do you think that I am?" There is no word, thought, or sentence in all four Gospels that does not have specific reference to answering this question. Each evangelist has written his Gospel in the hope that the reader will come to the same conclusion that he has, namely, that Jesus is the Christ, the Son of God.

Finding one literary category into which all four Gospels fit might be difficult. There is nothing in the ancient literature, including that of the first century A. D., that even nearly resembles them. The safest way to describe them each is as a "Gospel" that is, a book written to convince people about who Jesus really is. They could also be called theologies. The authors are men of definite convictions concerning divine matters. For years it was said, sometimes without too much thought, that the Gospels were not "dogmatics" or theological textbooks. Pushing aside all the unfavorable images connected with the word dogmatic, the term dogmatics might be the best in expressing what the authors wrote.

If the reader of a Gospel cannot accept the evangelist's own convictions about Jesus, he will be totally blind and ignorant in determining the literary intent of the Gospel. Such a reader might understand the meaning of the individual words and the grammatical forms. He might be able to trace the ancient meaning of the words and appreciate their linguistic usage, but he will not fully appreciate the intent of the Gospel. But the Scriptures are not alone in demanding this claim. Every writing can be better understood when the author's intentions become clear. It is with this frame of mind that we will answer the question: "What do you think of Jesus?"

There are four gospels; Matthew, Mark, Luke, and John, which claim to tell us about Jesus. Each is written with the purpose of bringing the reader to the conviction that Jesus is God's one answer for all men, but each writer does it in a different way. If the church had only one gospel, she would have sufficient knowledge about Jesus. However, God has provided four accounts of His ministry. Each is a road that brings us to Jesus. Most Christians have traveled all four roads, and at the end each have found a Savior. No unanimity exists in the church about which is the best. The writers had different personalities, so it is natural that some readers would be attracted to one more than to another. The diversity is an advantage and not a hindrance.

It cannot be said with certainty which Gospel was the earliest. Many prominent scholars today favor Mark as the earliest since it is the shortest, and most of the material he records can be found in Matthew and Luke. However, this theory is not without difficulties. John was always considered the last, but some scholars now are favoring an earlier date for his Gospel. I have chosen the Gospel of Matthew as a kind of prime guide to find Jesus, not because I am absolutely certain that this was the first Gospel, but because it comes from Palestine, the land where Jesus lived. Where necessary the other three Gospels will be cited. They are all reliable. The tradition of the church from the first century generally considered it the first and it was placed in our canon this way. Mark was always associated with Rome and like Luke and Acts was probably written from the same city. These men were probably not prominently associated with Jesus' ministry. John spent the last years of his life on the island of Patmos, an island off the coast of Asia Minor. Matthew was with Jesus during His ministry and wrote his Gospel in Palestine. This Gospel breathes the Jewish air. These are not arguments for the absolute priority of this Gospel but rather reasons for choosing it. Matthew wrote his Gospel closer to the places where Jesus actually lived. Many things might have changed between the lifetime of Jesus and when Matthew wrote them down. Still, like Jesus, he was a Jew who lived in Palestine, and they both enjoyed the same cultural climate. Besides, Matthew contains more details about the one important episode in which Jesus raised the question: "Who do you say that I am?"

CHAPTER II

Introducing Jesus

The Beginnings

Americans pride themselves in asserting the equality of all men in regard to the opportunities that are open to them. This democratic way of thinking is still new in the world. Kings and other hereditary princes still reign in many European countries and principalities, even though their direct influence in government has been waning since the last century. Great Britain, which is the home of Western democracy, through a parliamentary system as we have it in the United States, still has the House of Lords where many of the members possess their titles and offices through inheritance.

In America names still count in politics and business. Young men with names like Eisenhower, Stevenson, Kennedy, Rockefeller will have a better chance to succeed than the average man. Political groups, businesses, and even churches have their built-in dynasties. The pastor's son might be an average "Joe," still the congregation regards him differently. More is expected of him.

The Jews had a strong consciousness of hereditary rights which were not only protected by their deep-seated traditions but also by their laws. Property had to stay within the family, even when it was sold. Only descendants of Aaron could be priests. Temple functions could only be performed by members of the tribe of Levi. Since the kingdom of Judah fell to the Babylonians around 600 B.C., the Jews had Persians, Greeks, and Romans for rulers, but only a true descendant of David could really be *the* king. The Jews took very seriously the promise of God that the throne could only belong to David's family.

From the moment of His conception, Jesus was *Somebody* because of His family connections. Jesus' genealogy tells us that we can really expect *something* of Him. Matthew begins His Gospel with 42 segments of Jesus' family tree, 14 of which are full-blooded kings. Many people with good intentions of reading the Bible from cover to cover don't get too far beyond the first cover when they run smack up against one of those long genealogies for which the Old Testament is famous. Try as they may, most people cannot see their way clear through the hard-pronouncing names of Hebrew genealogy, with the sad result that they put the whole Bible aside. Genealogies are one of the most maligned and underrated forms of literature, at least in the Bible. Just from reading Jesus' pedigree we already have a clue to the question of who He really is.

First of all, the genealogy tells us that Jesus is a king. This thought will be found everywhere throughout all the Gospels — right up to His crucifixion. Along with the names of the 14 kings, there are the names of the 14 forefathers of the kings and the names of 14 descendants of the kings. The last 14 had the right to the crown, but never had the privilege of exercising it. When the Jews think of "king," they don't think first of Saul or Solomon or Josiah or anyone else, they think of David. The Old Testament, in sizing up a king, judges him against David, who was a model of faith. Bad kings are unlike David and good kings are like him in putting their trust solely in God.

Since the time of David, the Jews looked messianically at all of David's descendants. Solomon, for example, never really lived up to the high expectations that were associated with his coronation. Of course the Old Testament contains the story of how all of David's descendants failed to live up to God's Messianic expectations. In fact David himself failed. Since the reign of David, the Old Testament prophets spoke increasingly of a perfect king and a perfect kingdom. Jesus' royal genealogy means that in Him all of Israel's expectations for a perfect king find their culmination. The genealogy means that Jesus is the perfect product of the Messianic line.

There are other clues in the genealogy — slight but indicative of who Jesus is going to be. Look carefully at the genealogy and you will see the names of two Gentiles: Rahab and Ruth. Frequently the Jews had forgotten that they are the means of God's salvation and not the final goal. Abraham was to be a blessing to all the nations of the earth. His was to be an inclusive — not an exclusive relationship. Just as Jesus was descended from the Gentiles according to the flesh, so He would also include the Gentiles in His work. Rahab and Ruth are shadows of the Syro-Phoenician woman who stood head and shoulders above all God's "chosen people." Uriah, who is not a progenitor, but whose name is included, prepares the way for the two Roman centurions mentioned for their faith. The Gentiles are going to sit down in heaven with the patriarchal chiefs, Abraham, Isaac, and Jacob. Yes, Jesus' ministry is to the Jews only for the purpose of using them to make disciples out of all the nations.

Look again at Matthew's genealogy and you will see the name of three adulteresses: Tamar, Rahab, and Bathsheba (whom Matthew identifies not by her name but as the wife of Uriah). Jesus comes from sinners to save sinners. The harlots who trust in God enter the kingdom before the righteous who trust in themselves. Jesus not only embraces the sin of the future, but also the sin of the past, even when that sin belongs to His own ancestors.

The Announcement

Even before the actual conception of Jesus, who He was going to be and what He was going to do was being clearly spelled out. From the Old Testament we know that this is a usual way in which God prepares for the birth of men whom He intends to do great things for Him. Frequently the births of prominent people are preceded by angelic visits. Angels come to Abraham and Manoah to announce the births of Isaac and Samson. The angelic notification to Joseph concerning the birth of Jesus only furthers the thought that Jesus is to be a leader in Israel. Luke centers the prenatal angelic activity on Mary, while Matthew records the visit to Joseph. This is hardly accidental. Inheritance, especially the royal inheritance of David's throne, could only be given through the male. The family name could only be preserved through the male. It is through Joseph that Jesus is entitled to David's name and throne.

What's in a Name?

Most newlyweds take the naming of their children very seriously. Frequently children are named to honor the father or another relative. Sometimes names are given simply because they are in vogue. A name popular 20 or 30 years ago is hardly popular any more today. Names can thus be a clue to the general time of birth. A name may also be given because of the way it sounds together with the family name or because of the pleasant association it suggests with another person who also had the name.

Practically all names have meanings. The Jews were very conscious of the meanings of names and their historical association with great figures of the past. The name was to be prophetic of the child who bore it — or at least the parents hoped it would be. When God gives a name by direct revelation it is always prophetic of the child's destiny. The name "Jesus" was not an uncommon name among the Jews. It is like the Old Testament name Joshua and means "Yahweh is my salvation," or "God saves." The etymological meaning of the name is reenforced by the angel's interpretation that Jesus "will save His people from their sins." Other children had been called Jesus, but only the Son of Mary would actually live up to this name.

The Book of Leviticus contains very exact material on how the Jews were to indicate their penitential attitude to God and man through a sacrificial system. For the Jews, God and God only was the Redeemer of Israel. He called the Jews out of Egypt and made them a nation, and He alone came to the aid of the individual believer. With the name "Jesus" and the angelic interpretation that He would save *His* people from their sins, the angel identifies the unborn child of Mary as God Himself, as only God could redeem Israel. The child is to be called Jesus, not only because He would save His people from their sins but because the prophet Isaiah had said the virgin's son would be called Emmanuel.

Jesus means God saves and Emmanuel means God is with us, but the difference in meaning is only apparent as both names have the same significance. The God of the Old Testament is never just cultically present like the pagan gods. He is not confined to shrines. His presence cannot be mechanically brought about through incantations. Neither is the name Emmanuel, God is with us, merely a belief in the omnipresence of God. When God is present, He is more than *just* there, but out of freedom He chooses to be where He wants *for* the salvation of man. In the Old Testament, God chose to be present in victory and defeat, grace and judgment. For the true God to be present with His people means that He is present for the express purpose of saving His people, even when He is subsequently rejected. The Lord of hosts is present with Ahaz and his people to give them victory over their political enemies and with Jesus and His people to give them victory over the internal enemies of sin and death. Emmanuel, "God is with us," means Jesus, that is, God, is saving now.

The Virgin Conceived

The virgin birth of Jesus has always attracted a fair amount of theological attention. To conclude that modern 20th-century man cannot accept conception of Jesus by a virgin because of current biological studies is inane and disrespectful of human intelligence. Even the most unlettered peoples, ancient or modern, are fully aware that virgins do not give birth to children. From the very beginning the church has been attacked because of this doctrine that Jesus was born of a woman without the aid of man. The Ebionites, a Jewish-Christian sect, dating at least as far back as the Council of Jerusalem around the year 45 A. D., did not acknowledge this supernatural birth. In the second century a learned Egyptian aristocrat, Celsus by name, vehemently inveighed against it. He offered the opinion that Mary had become pregnant by a German soldier in the employ of the Roman armies stationed in Palestine. In the last century many Protestant scholars revived these theories and added new ones of their own to account for the birth of Jesus.

Most prominent theologians who bear the name Lutheran today, including many who are conservatively inclined, have attempted to give a natural explanation to the miraculous birth of Jesus. They claim that the accounts of the virgin birth as we have them in the Gospels of Matthew and Luke were invented in early Christian congregations where there was a strong Hellenistic-Roman or Egyptian influence. In the Hellenistic-Roman world great men were at times said to be born of virgins. Since Jesus was divine, it was quite natural to say that the church, out of a sense of deep piety and without maliciousness, added the legendary elements of a virgin birth to His life. The Egyptians knew of legends in which their gods had intercourse with virgins. This also might account for the Biblical record, according to this school of thought. Some Christians confronted with these and similar arguments have meekly and cowardly surrendered by asserting that the important thing is that God was active in Jesus. But do we have the right to give up the virgin birth or any other supernatural truth which has been revealed by God through the Scriptures? The virgin birth might not be the first thing to be preached to the unbelieving world, but it is part of the teaching of "all things" for every believer who wants to grow in the knowledge of His Lord and salvation. Just as the empty tomb is the sign that Jesus had been exalted by God, so the virgin birth is the sign that Jesus really is Emmanuel. "God with us." Virgin birth and resurrection are brackets around the life of Jesus authenticating His person and work. Signs are important not in themselves, but because of what they signify.

The Gospels of Matthew and Luke are the only ones which give us the account of the birth of Jesus. Each contains different elements, but both are agreed that Jesus was born of Mary alone without a human father. There are, however, other parts of the New Testament Scriptures that teach that God is the Father of Jesus, without alluding to or suggesting a human father. In Galatians 4:4 Paul mentions that God sent His Son born of a woman. No mention is made of a human father. If there had been one, Paul would surely have mentioned him. In the preceding chapter he notes that Abraham had two sons. This would have given Paul a fine opportunity to mention Joseph or someone else. Jewish genealogy and descent is through the father and not the mother. No respectable Jew would trace birth through a man's mother, unless as in the case of Jesus who had no human father. When the Jews called Him "Jesus, the son of Joseph" (John 6:42), He begins to speak about God as His Father. The account of the child Jesus in the temple (Luke 2:41-51) also shows that God is the real Father of Jesus. When Mary scolds Him for troubling her and "your father", i. e., Joseph, Jesus responds that He had to be about His Father's business.

These pericopes indicate that Jesus in His own lifetime, at least according to what the evangelists have recorded, was aware of and sensitive about His unique birth of a woman alone, and on at least two occasions He spoke directly to the issue. The early church, as soon as it began preaching about Jesus, shared in this sensitivity and included it in its basic teaching from the beginning. The Christians felt very defensive about the resurrection of Jesus also and had to defend themselves on this point. Matthew tells us about how the Jews circulated a story that His resurrection could be accounted for by the stealing of His body by the disciples (28:11-15). Undoubtedly they were spreading slanderous remarks about Mary. Never once does Matthew dare suggest that these slanders had any truth in them at all, but he does direct the gaze of the Jews to their own royal house. Solomon, Israel's wisest king, had been born of the adulterer king, David, and an army captain's adulterous wife, Bathsheba.

Matthew's Gospel simply and convincingly bears witness that Mary is with child by the Holy Spirit. As God's Son, born of a virgin, He would soon be again attacked by Satan, the archenemy of God.

27

CHAPTER III

Jesus Versus Satan:
Who Will Win?

Right after Jesus had been ordained by John's baptism into His work of standing in man's place before God, He headed straight for the wilderness to meet Satan. At His baptism His Father had outfitted Jesus with the Spirit for this conflict. God's Spirit directed Jesus because God had unsettled business and a score to settle with Satan. In all of Jesus' Messianic work, the Spirit would assist Him. The unknown writer of the Letter to the Hebrews states that the Spirit stuck with Jesus to the very end and even helped Him offer the sacrifice to the Father for the world's sin. Many of God's people had possessed God's Spirit in one way or another, but the mark of the Messiah was that He would have the Spirit without measure.

The wilderness was not really the first place where Jesus had met Satan. Already in His infancy, God's Son was being stalked by that diabolical creature that Peter would later call a lion on the prowl. When the world was first created, Satan had used a serpent to do his dirty work. Now Herod the Great, who had tried to exterminate God's Messiah as an infant, was the instrument in Satan's foul play. Herod had all the marks of Satanic domination. He acted just like you would expect Satan to act. He planned for the death of God's Messiah under the pretense that he wanted to worship Him. At least this is what he told the Magi from the East. Satan can always be "found at prayer." (Paul says the man of perdition sits right in the middle of God's temple.) When Herod's cunning plans are thwarted, his cool temperament becomes furiously hot. The calculating murderer becomes an enraged butcher commanding the execution of all boys in Bethlehem under the age of two. But this is one of the "sacramental" marks of Satan's kingdom—killing saints. Jesus Himself says that Satan was a murderer from the beginning. At that time he had entered the heart of Cain to kill Abel.

Satan has always played a crucial role in the crisis periods of God's history, and he has always found willing and ready collaborators. On this earth it often looks like Satan has the upper hand, and it is God's people who fight from the position of weakness. All men are naturally his allies, and logistics is never a problem for him. By a miraculous turn of events the infant Jesus escapes from Herod's armies in almost the same way that the infant Moses eluded the armies of Pharaoh, who also was another willing agent of Satan.

The episode between Jesus and Satan in the wilderness is just one more conflict between heaven and hell. Some well-known theologians have considered this continuous battle as one of might against might and muscle against muscle. If this were the case, then God would have the upper hand. All He would really have to do is to speak a word from His almighty power and that would be the end of it; but He is also a God of justice.

God is opposed to Satan, because He hates sin. Sin is never impersonal. Every sin in one way or another has its origins in Satan and is therefore a deliberate and personal affront to God. It is man's rebellion in the sense of the First Commandment of not letting God be God. Jesus conquers Satan not with thunderbolts from heaven but with actions that completely conform to God's will. Satan is defeated when Jesus shows him that there is a *Man* who gives Himself fully and totally to God and does not succumb to satanic rebellion like Adam and his descendants had done and are still doing.

Jesus meets Satan in the wilderness. He was physically weakened by hunger caused by a 40-day fast, but He was ready for the conflict since He nourished His inner life on God's bread, His Word. The desert conflict is a double exposure on a film that already had recorded another conflict in which Adam and Eve,

God's first representatives, had lost a significant battle to Satan. The lush garden has been exchanged for a barren desert, still the second exposure fits comfortably over the first. Satan uses the same tactical procedure of quoting Scripture but with a slight change of wording and thus a twist of meaning. The big difference was that in Eden Satan quotes the words of God once and wins. In the desert he quotes three times and loses.

Satan's causes always look religious, and in fact they are, at least outwardly. In Genesis 3 he quotes from the words of God in Genesis 2 but with a slight switch in the wording. "You may freely eat of any tree of the garden except the tree of life," becomes "Did God say, 'You shall not eat of any tree of the garden'?" This might qualify as the first theological question. Herod, who is truly "Anti-Christ" because he desires to defeat God's plans in the Messiah, to find the Child with the intention of destroying Him uses the very word that God Himself spoke through the prophet Micah. Of course, God eludes him.

With his superior religious and theological knowledge Satan always manages to play a prominent role at a significant juncture in God's history. Many battles will be fought and won by Jesus, but absolute victory will come only after the final conflict. Satan had attempted to kill the infant Messiah and lost. He attempted to dissuade Jesus from doing what God wanted Him to do; he tempted Him with a false messiahship centering in world rule and dominion. There were three parts to that battle: desert, temple, and mountain. Still all was not lost for Satan — victory for him could be grasped from the jaws of defeat with only one decisive battle. Somehow and in some way Jesus must still be kept away from that cross.

The high point of Messianic confession comes in Caesarea Philippi where Peter with emotive conviction asserts that Jesus is the Christ, the Son of the living God. Jesus then explains to His disciples that Messiahship means death for sin. This Peter will not allow. He calls upon the powers of heaven to direct Jesus along another path. Peter's help is labeled as satanic. "Get behind me, Satan! You are a hindrance to Me; for you are not on the side of God, but of men!" are as severe as any words spoken to any man. Satan had in fact used an emotionally freighted religious moment, when the disciples had reached a rare plateau of confessional commitment, to turn God's chief spokesman, Peter, against Him. This of course was a classic moment. Satan was even using Jesus' closest confidant and most promising disciple, the great confessor himself — Peter. God's adversary is very religious!

The final struggle and last battle would be suffering and crucifixion. The thought of death is not pleasant for any man; and a death for the sin and perversion of man is a horror. With these thoughts Jesus would wrestle in the Garden of Gethsemane. If Jesus would sidestep the cross and remain in the cool recesses of the garden, Satan could chalk up two "garden victories," Eden and Gethsemane. Jesus left that garden willingly so Adam and his kind could return to a better Paradise than that from which they had been once expelled.

The traces of Satan's vain attempts to overthrow God can be seen everywhere in the Gospels. The main conflicts have already been indicated: Herod's persecution, the temptation, Peter's confession, and the Lord's final agony. Other imprints of satanic determination show up here and there in the Gospels.

The account of the temptation is not only a preview of the Garden of Gethsemane, but the 40 days are a haunting reminder of the 40 years that the Jews had to spend in the wilderness because of their own rebellion. They had failed to believe and follow God's directives. That's about as clear and concise a definition of sin as you can get. God had once called to His son, "Israel," in Egypt to come out — and he didn't listen. His penalty was a 40-year trip in the wilderness. Jesus had listened. The "Second Israel" would not like the first let Satan successfully intervene.

Everywhere in the ministry of Jesus, devils, Satan's loyal and faithful cohorts, are sticking their fiendish heads into Jesus' Messianic business. Being accomplished theologians they salute Jesus as the Son of God in the country of the Gadarenes and are given festive exit in a local herd of pigs. They know that they are eschatologically doomed, and they suggest to Jesus that they still are entitled to a little more time for their devilish delights (Matt. 8:28-34). (Let the reader of the New Testament find and study for himself the cases where Jesus deals mercifully with the demoniacs, those miserable people who have become mechanical dupes for Satan.) Wherever Jesus meets the demon possessed, there is open conflict.

Much more treacherous, though not as exciting, is where Satan and his cohorts try to get tangled up with the church, a place where they most frequently succeed. They literally come out of church walls. (This is called in the wide sense, the doctrine of the kingdom of the Anti-Christ, whose members have hearts which belong to Satan, but outwardly they have acceptable religious markings.) Jesus told the parables of the tares and the wheat and the good and bad fish (Matthew 13) to alert His faithful that Satan conducts two battles against the church — one from the outside and another from within. The latter is conducted with all kinds of religious paraphernalia.

This is part of Satan's scheme to make the godless look godly, and the godly look godless. Not even Jesus, God's own representative, was exempt from this particular satanic tactic. Matthew 12:22-32 is a classic account of how this confusion can take place. A thrice-cursed man is brought to Jesus. He is blind, incapable of speaking, and worst of all he is possessed with a demon. The poor man is relieved of all his ailments, and the people witnessing the divine miracle suggest that perhaps Jesus is the Son of David, God's own Messiah, the man to deliver all men. This confession of faith receives the unfavorable retort from the Pharisees, the popular religious leaders of the common people, that Jesus is in league with Beelzebul, the prince of demons. No one is exempt from Satan's clever maneuver — not even God's Son.

But wasn't this a replay of another sort? Even before the 'beginning' Satan had tried to arouse his angelic colleagues in blasphemous battle against God, replacing God with Satan. This is how sin began, and it is a history that can be easily traced in the Testaments right up to the time that Jesus died.

In the Old Testament, the Lord God's major opponent among His people is Baal, a prominent deity among the resident tribes of Palestine. From the time of Moses on, the Israelites shared some of God's praise with Baal. A constantly recurring theme in the preaching of the prophets of the Old Testament was the choice that the people had to make between God and Baal. A Jewish name for Satan, Beelzebul, is etymologically related to God's most prominent opponent, Baal. To say that Jesus was in league with Beelzebul was like saying that Jesus endorsed the idolatrous worship of the unbelievers. It was like saying that instead of being the incarnate God, Jesus was the incarnate Satan.

The name of Satan or the devil is written across every page of world history. The struggle between him and God is also the unwritten agenda on every page of the Bible. To be sure, the world is interested in the eradication of evil, but evil is treated like some chemical imbalance that can be corrected by the right proportions of legislation, education, and money. Satan is relegated to a costume party at a masquerade. "You little devil, you!" a phrase used with little boys who are not what we think they should be, is about as serious as most people get about the matter.

Jesus was dead serious about Satan. All the world's misery could be traced directly back to him. Human affliction and disease all have their origin in the recesses of his mind. Thrown from God's presence, he takes great delight in capturing God's saints and turning them into his own devotees. Wherever Jesus preached God's kingdom, whenever He healed people and raised them from the dead, whenever people believed in Jesus and switched their allegiance to God, there Jesus was delivering death blows against Satan's kingdom.

The crucifixion of Jesus brought the entire matter to a head. Satan can be found throughout the entire story: in the traitorous act of Judas (John tells us that Satan entered his heart); in the cowardly actions of the disciples; in the bloodthirsty cries of the crowd; in the trials; in the nails and thorns—everywhere. This was one drama where the producer and director were the same person—Satan! Even though God was in those moments in retreat, Paul tells us that He was in fact disarming Satan of His favorite weapons. Satan directs man to sin and then uses these same sins to accuse us in God's presence. He leads us to sin, troubles our conscience with our sin, and then informs God about them. Jesus nailed our sins to His cross and thereby gave Satan no basis to accuse God's saints. "The old evil foe," as Luther calls him in the hymn "A Mighty Fortress," is still making all sorts of grunts. His threats are foreboding — but the poor fellow is fighting without his weapons. "His bark is worse than his bite."

Jesus described the conflict between Himself and Satan in very colorful terms in the parable of the strong man. Satan, a mighty man, is safely sequestered in his fortress with the souls of mankind as his dear possession. Jesus, with a more impressive array, lays siege to Satan's ramparts which till then stood there impregnable to every moral attempt of man to ascend them. With His cross Jesus has stripped Satan of his protection. The Christian church calls Christ's victory ending this deadly strife, the only truly "cosmic" battle the world has ever known, since the world itself hung in the balance, the "descent into hell."

After His crucifixion and when assuming His body again, Jesus paraded triumphantly in hell, on Satan's home territory. What this "looked" like cannot be described with our terms of reference. Some Christian artists have done a marvelous job in depicting it on canvas. Common is the picture of Jesus standing on the grave or before the open tomb with the battle scars visible in hands, feet, and side, indicating the reality of the conflict, and with the banner of the cross in His hand, an ensign of victory flown over Satan's very own country.

The church, the people who belong to God and have Jesus as their leader, is engaged now in a kind of mopping up action. Jesus has captured Satan's main fortress. The enemy still lingers in the outposts of the hearts of men. He cannot be moved by military steel or elaborate church programs or money, regardless of the source. The weapon is still the same Word Jesus used. Wherever and whenever the Word is spoken, and allegiance is switched from Satan to God, heaven is only perfecting its victory over hell. Remember how Jesus told us about the angels who cheer every time somebody repents.

The full end of this story of the conflict between God's champion, Christ Jesus, and hell's antagonist, Satan, cannot be told on these pages simply because many minibattles are aflame in the hearts of men. Jesus did however give us an outline of what was to come. God has appointed a time when all the enemy will be rounded up and safely put away. Till that day comes, the church wins men for God and from Satan by telling them that they now belong to God through what Jesus did on the cross. Of course this is exactly what Jesus did in His own preaching.

A word of caution can be directed at the church. On a number of occasions, Jesus' disciples wanted to attack His enemies with actual military weapons made of steel. The Lord patiently put His overzealous friends in their places. Today some very sincere Christians are looking forward to the military victory of the modern nation of Israel. Still others expect the government through appropriate legislation to bring about a glorious kingdom on earth. If only the solution were that simple! Satan will not be touched by these kinds of approaches. In fact these people fall right into his hands. According to the parables of Jesus, it will be the angels who will carry out the final plans of execution. The only sword that the church has against Satan is "the sword of the Spirit which is the Word of God."

CHAPTER IV

Jesus and the Wrath of God

Hell

Maybe instead of speaking about wrath, another theological and Biblical term, familiar to practically everybody, should be used—hell. This is hardly the place for a lecture on its regular use in the English language. Modern man might have advanced 'n many areas, but he still shows a predilection for the word's use in such a variety of ways, so staggering the linguistic imagination that it approaches the status of being the universal word in our speech. (The propriety of the printed page prevents giving examples.)

Hell is the kind of subject that forces itself into most discussions about religion. Somewhere tucked away in the back corners of the human mind is the idea of hell. — Unbelievers not excluded. The way people get around the haunting scepter of hell's prince, whose presence is more faithful than our own shadows, is to assert that hell is something that people create for themselves on earth. This thought recurs with faithful precision wherever people talk about religion. All this business about countering "hell on earth" is hardly more than whistling in the dark. Man has created plenty of "hells" for himself on this earth. Calling a place or a situation "a living hell" is frequently an apt and appropriate expression. But limiting hell to earth is really only a game that people play. The thought of hell on earth is much more tolerable than facing hell after death. A hell on earth has to end. The same cannot be said with any confidence about hell after death.

A hell after this life is so uncomfortable not only to the average man but also to many professional theologians that many religions have tried to dispose of the whole nasty business.

The Mormons teach that man has another chance after life. The Jehovah's Witnesses—and they are followed by many main line Christians in this respect—teach that annihilation and not hell is the fate of those who do not follow their doctrines. Annihilation or a return to nonexistence is preferable to the torturous existence of hell. Jesus even said of Judas, as He thought of his fate in hell, that it would have been better if that traitorous disciple had never been born.

Many theologians in the last 200 years have influenced the major denominations with their ideas that hell has no real existence but that it belongs to the inventions of man's creative imagination. Many hybrids of this type of thinking can be readily found. One of the most popular is that God is so loving that He would hardly hold men responsible for their mistakes. In this type of thinking Jesus dies not to take away sin and its awful consequences but to alleviate man's consciousness of guilt. Jesus dies to show man that everything is all right. His death is hardly more than an object lesson. (One can imagine more fitting object lessons.) For others hell is simply symbolical of men's alienation from God or from each other. At worst, "Hell is other people."

God's Wrath (Otherwise Known as Hell)— The Overarching Reality

Everywhere in our New Testament, God's wrath or personal anger over sin is written in capital letters. It is the backdrop without which the mission of Jesus can never be understood. The angelic message to Joseph about Mary's Son states that the Child is going to save His people from their sins. This does not mean that with the appearance of Jesus, people are going to stop sinning. It does mean that He is going to save them from the hellish consequences of their sin. Sin carries with it the idea of penalty, liability to punishment. It's the penalty of sin that frightens people. This motivates them to shove hell under the rug or to exchange it for something less unpleasant. Death and hell are sin's ultimate penalties. Even for the day-to-day "little sins" the cause and effect principle is at work.

The Mosaic Code, especially as it is found in the Books of

Exodus and Deuteronomy, prescribes specific penalties for specific sins. For us who are removed by time and culture from the ancient Israelites, the cadence of sin and punishment might be both uninteresting and inappropriate. Still God was teaching the lesson with loud and clear words that sin is a real offence to Him and that the penalty must be extracted. If we avoid it, we do so only for a time. Sin's penalty is inevitable. Even the world quips that we can only be sure of two things: death and taxes. The guilt of sin has more reality than a psychological disturbance.

The idea that sin demands payment is hardly foreign to the Gospels. The woman caught in adultery faces the prospect of stoning. Jesus questions not the propriety of her fate, but the qualifications of the executioners who should be destined to the same reward. Judas is fully conscious of perpetrating the death of an innocent man and knows that for his part in this murder, his own life must be forfeited. The principle of a life for a life is still valid. By returning the money to the priests he attempts to pay the penalty for treacherously taking an innocent life. Even precious metals are never sufficient payment for human life. By suicide he attempts to follow Moses' directives to make atonement for the *one* act, but hardly for all the acts for which God still holds him accountable. The famous question of Peter of how many times he must forgive his brother contains the haunting reminder that sooner or later each man is held accountable for his own actions. The reply of Jesus, that forgiveness should be an infinite quality in Christians, does not suggest that God does not exact a penalty for sin, but rather that since God has provided the payment of the penalty further restitution demanded by Christians is not only unnecessary but even offensive to God.

The Jews at Jesus' time were very conscious of the cause and effect relationship between sin and punishment. At one time His disciples asked Jesus whether a certain man's blindness was caused by his own sin or his parents'. They had interpreted the man's blindness, rightly or wrongly, as a penalty for a specific sin which they were trying to pinpoint. The Book of Job is a series of conversations discussing *what* sin Job had done to earn such calamities.

The relationship between sin and God's wrath as it manifests itself in specific punishments and the more general punishment of hell gives essential meaning to the death of Jesus. Many have offered other explanations for the death of Jesus. Here are several examples: Jesus died to show us that God is not angry and that we don't have to fear death, even the most torturous; Jesus died because He was considered by the Roman occupation forces as an insurrectionist; Jesus died because he threatened to destroy the ecclesiastical establishment; Jesus died because He interpreted this as His fate; it was the inevitable. The last one is the message of *Jesus Christ Superstar*. To this could be added many other explanations. These opinions — some containing perhaps even more than a grain of truth — should not obscure the real cause of His death, God's wrath over sin as God placed it on Jesus. This is the message of the four Gospels and attested to by the other New Testament writings.

"Giving Them Hell"
The Concept of Wrath in the Preaching
of John and Jesus

Before Jesus had begun His public ministry, John the Baptizer, Jesus' forerunner, preached on the wrath of God in such a way that it reminded the people of the preaching of many of the Old Testament prophets, especially Elijah. Men like Elijah were associated with the destruction of the Kingdom of Israel, the Ten Tribes, by the Assyrians, and the deportation of Judah by the Babylonians. Theirs was a message with teeth and there was no doubt in the people's mind that when God spoke His message of wrath through His prophets, He meant business!

It is no wonder that when John appeared in the wilderness around the Jordan there was a mass exodus that crossed the denominational boundaries of that time. The Judeans could not forget that their brothers in the north had once been removed from God's presence by permanent exportation and that their own capital city of Jerusalem had been reduced to ashes by foreign hordes around the year 600 B. C. Their own ancestors had been forced to live in Babylonia.

John immediately suspected the motives of those who flocked into the river for baptism. Were they coming for baptism because they believed sincerely that they had offended God by their lives; or was it only an insurance policy against divine extermination? The fiery preacher hardly greeted them with open arms. Here was one "congregation" which demanded more of the applicant than that he sign a yellow card professing that he sincerely loves the Lord Jesus. He called them snakes, children not of God but of that creature in whom Satan had become incarnate. Later Jesus called them snakes right to their faces.

People are not 'just bad.' They are agents of Satan; and God's wrath zeroes in on the person and on his allegiance to Satan. When God's wrath appears, all status relationships disappear. Abraham's sons can be replaced by stones. They have the marks of religiosity as far as men are concerned, but with God they have registered only negatively. They are headed for the fire.

Like it or not, God's wrath is associated with fire. Little wonder that a common English expression indicates the intensity of heat with the words: "hot as hell." Both John and Jesus use the word fire to express God's final eschatological displeasure over man's rebellion. However, the thought is not new with them. In the Old Testament psalms, for example, God's anger burns. Zephaniah states that "in the fire of His jealous wrath all the earth shall be consumed." Malachi compares the day of judgment with the heat of a burning oven. When fire is used of God's wrath, it means the destruction or removal of what God considers offensive to Him.

John introduced the 'fire' concept of God's wrath into the New Testament preaching. Trees cut down faced further destruction in fire. As fiery as John was, he promised that the message of Jesus would be even more severe. John preached about the fire, but Jesus would burn all those opposed to Him with what John calls "the unquenchable fire." Jesus lived up to all of John's expectations. The tares, the people who have the marks of Christians but really are not, are consigned to the fire. Those who have not done good to the least of Jesus' brethren are told to go to the eternal fire. Chorazin and Capernaum are to face a fate worse than Sodom's. That city with Gomorrah was literally burned alive by fire in Abraham's day. Some archeologists assert these two ancient cities lie beneath the Dead Sea. In the parable of the wedding feast for the king's son, those who refuse the invitation have their cities burned. Such preaching was not wasted on the Jews.

Fire is not the only way God's wrath is described in the New Testament. Equally effective is the idea of separation from God. John told the Pharisees and Sadducees that without a sincere change in their lives, they would be cut off from God's people in spite of their blood relationship to Abraham. The workers in the parable of the vineyard are given a one-way ticket out of their possession—almost in the style of Adam and Eve's exit from Eden's garden. Those who have not acted positively to the least of Jesus' brethren hear the gruesome verdict: "Depart." The parables of the net and the tares teach the same lesson: separation from God's righteous ones.

Hell's fire, whatever else it involves, provides no light. Already in the Old Testament, the day of the Lord's eschatological judgment is one of "deep darkness." Believing Gentiles bask with Abraham and the patriarchs in eternal light. Unbelieving Jews, whom Jesus calls the "sons of the kingdom," are to be thrown into the outer darkness. The guest without the wedding garment faces a similar doom.

Perhaps the most uncomfortable feature of God's wrath is its eternal quality. Many Christians, some of them quite sincere, have tried to get around this. Yet the preaching of Jesus leaves little doubt about hell's durable quality. Jesus never speaks about the second chance. The fire that burns does not go out. The unforgiving servant is imprisoned and can obtain no release till he pays all. Of course this can never happen.

God's chief agent in carrying out His wrath and managing hell is Satan, who receives adequate assistance from His own angels. All who have rebelled against God or who have refused to repent deserve each other. The presence of evil in this world is a mystery. Philosophers have tried to explain it but with no success. The Bible explains it as the traitorous act of men and angels, both of whom were made somewhat like God Himself and

41

whom God had even taken into His confidence. Strange as it might seem, God uses His most eminent opponent, Satan, to execute wrath and judgment. He is thus an instrument in God's hand and under His control.

Many other things could be said about God's wrath, but some of its chief characteristics according to the preaching of John and Jesus can be recapped here: It is associated with fire. It involves separation from God and His chosen people. It cloaks its victims with an eternal shroud of darkness. It never ends. Satan is active in carrying out God's wrath.

Only when God's wrath is understood in such strong terms does the task of Jesus of Nazareth become clearer. No words can adequately describe God's wrath, but it would be to this indescribable wrath that Jesus would submit Himself. In connection with the words of John, Jesus says that all righteousness must be fulfilled. In His baptism Jesus puts Himself in the sinners' place. Not only does He do what they should have done, but He suffers the penalties for what they have done.

The Hidden Agenda

The death of Jesus of Nazareth some time around the A. D. 27 was not a particularly shattering event so far as most of his contemporaries were concerned. It was business as usual on the next morning and the next morning and so on. Just one more politically dangerous person had been put away by the authorities. It is common practice to get rid of the troublemaker when a situation promises to get out of hand. It wasn't so many years ago that the Soviet Union quietly and still deliberately took from the public eye the popular First Secretary of the Communist Party in Czechoslovakia, Alexander Dubcek.

Back in the first century, Pontius Pilate and the high priests acted in a similar way. Jesus was a troublemaker that simply had to be disposed of. We could even suppose that they had had previous experience in handling political mavericks. Stepping over, around and even *on* people is still the way to get to the top — *and to stay there!* The words of the high priest Caiaphas, in John's Gospel, that Jesus should die to insure their positions and to prevent further Roman intervention, are classic to this very day. "It is expedient that one man should die for the people!" The threats of the crowd against Pilate that he would be no friend of Caesar's unless he brought death to the Nazarene are just part of a lesson in practical politics. The dripping hands of Pilate over the wash basin teach that for this world political power is more important than the question of right and wrong, guilt and innocence. But more was at stake in the death of this "rebel" than the political careers of a governor and a few wheeling and dealing priests.

For this occasion there were two audiences. While the Jewish and Roman authorities seemed fully in charge on Golgatha's Hill—it had gone better than their fondest hopes—God was not only watching the events, He was the prime director. Hidden beneath the arrest, trials, and crucifixion of the Teacher from Galilee was God's own agenda. John in his Gospel explains that the high priest's words about the expedience of one man's death for the people really meant that all people in all times could benefit from it in an eternal way. Paul also speaks about God's 'hidden agenda.' The Jews and Romans would not have acted as they did, if they had known that they had the Lord of glory on their hands.

Who then is responsible for Jesus' death—God or the Jews and Romans? This is not the place to put first-century sinners on trial. Peter told Jerusalem's inhabitants that they were guilty of the crime, and many of them felt sorry for their actions and repented. Others went to their death stubbornly asserting their innocence in the face of the evidence. Let the matter rest there. The Jew today is no more guilty of Jesus' death than the Christian. Church verdicts absolving Jewish guilt for Jesus' death are at best hypocritical.

For the moment we have to push through the events of that Friday in early April some time around the A. D. 27 to see what was happening so far as God was concerned. According to all our Gospel accounts, Jesus knew what was going to happen to Him. He was in complete control of the situation. Just after Peter had confessed Jesus as God's Son, the Messiah, Jesus explained that the Messianic kingdom would come about through His death. "The Son of Man *must* go up to Jerusalem and be handed over to the chief priests."

The clue to the death of Jesus can be found in the word "must." This is not merely an inner compulsion or fanatical whim. Compulsive people get something on their mind that they have to *do* something; and they are not satisfied till it's done, even though there is no apparent necessity for the action. The "must" in Jesus' life is not from within but from without. It is a "must" that comes from God. Even before the world took its final shape, God had prepared an agenda that His Son would become a man and that His life would be a payment for sin. For thousands of years the world was writing its own history, but beneath every page God was bringing His own planning to completion. Secular historians never mention what God was doing — simply because they were not aware of God's plans. Empires, some whose names we know, like the Egyptian, the Assyrian, the Babylonian, the Greek, the Roman and others whose existence still lies hidden in the ruins of time, are all tools in God's hands, directed to bringing about what He considered the most important of occurrences, the appearance and death of His Son.

Jesus was fully aware of God's plans and accepted the divine obligation. Christians hearing about the death of Jesus are frequently filled with the emotion of righteous indignation at the death of an innocent man, wishing that it hadn't happened; we still try to second-guess God. Why didn't Jesus stay away from the authorities in Jerusalem and pursue a peaceful ministry in the north country of Galilee? Why did Jesus have to offend the ecclesiastical establishment? Jesus could have possibly avoided arrest in the Garden of Gethsemane. A miracle performed for Herod could have saved Him from the cross. A pledge of allegiance to Tiberius Caesar, the reigning Roman emperor, would have meant immediate release from custody and the end of a bloody business. All these are our thoughts, but not God's.

Without the death of the God-Man, mankind, this mass of humanity, would wallow in its own sin and drown. The justice and the love of God had written the word "must" over the death of Jesus. From God's point of view, it was unavoidable. Jesus had spoken about the irrevocable divine verdict of death that hung over His life right after Peter's confession. At least on two other occasions, Jesus would use virtually the same words. The disciples had to be prepared. Nothing had pleased the disciples, Peter, James, and John, more than what they had experienced on the Mount of Transfiguration. All of earth's problems and even its glories melt and evaporate in what heaven has to offer. If they could only stay there — but they can't. At least they couldn't stay then. Heaven could only be reached by going to Jerusalem and to the cross.

Again as Jesus made the final preparation to go into Jerusalem, the disciples anticipated the final glory. They were already dividing the spoils of God's kingdom among themselves and not without a fair amount of disagreement about who would get what. Jesus again must remind them that final glory comes only through His death by a cross. The disciples were looking forward to their rewards; but Jesus was reading God's hidden agenda. Right in the middle of this agenda were written the words: DEATH BY CRUCIFIXION.

The agenda that Jesus was following was not really so hidden or secretive. God had written it in the Old Testament. The problem was that God's people had read it but did not want to understand its full implications.

The Old Testament — The Hidden Agenda

There is no lack of Old Testament passages cited in the New. If the plans of God were hidden, they were hidden only to the world which does not take God at His word. God had spoken; the world had not listened. (This is an old business going back to Satan, Adam, and all the children of men.) At least for Jesus this is the way the Gospel writers, particularly Matthew, describe it. The Old Testament was God's blueprint, which permitted no deviation. It was like a musical score for a conductor. It gave the words of a play which set down the actions and the words of the actors very precisely.

On Thursday, when Jesus knew that the Father had given

the divine cue, He told His disciples that His hour had come. God had set the events of trial and crucifixion in process. There was no turning back now. Oh, yes, those historical figures were all playing a part, a part for which they would be held responsible, but it was the part that God had given them. "The Son of Man was going as it had been written of Him; but woe to that man by whom the Son of Man is betrayed." The Old Testament Scriptures were unfolding like a divine plot. Even the fickle nature of cowardly disciples came as no surprise. When the shepherd was struck down, the sheep would scatter. At least this is what one Old Testament prophet had said.

It was in the Garden of Gethsemane that Jesus reached the agonizing apex of what it meant to follow God's written directives. Three times He made a special petition to the Father to remove "the cup." This is a strange expression for us. What does it mean to take away a cup? Several of the Old Testament prophets, for example Jeremiah, Isaiah, and Ezekiel speak about the cup of God's wrath. God's fury is compared to being forced to drink a cup of wine in which the bitter-tasting particles sink to the bottom.

This was more than just a vivid expression of speech. It was used to describe how God would destroy the sacred city of Jerusalem and bring the independent nationhood of the elect people to an end. Just as God had rejected Israel, His chosen and now prodigal "son," God was planning to reject Jesus, His chosen and faithful Son. The role that should have been played by the first Israel was assumed by the Second Israel. (Since God has vented His furious wrath on Jesus, the cup of the Christian flows over with blessings. "My cup runneth over. Surely goodness and mercy shall follow me all the days of my life.")

At the end of these struggles, Jesus faces the divine inevitable. He signals the final act with the words: "Behold the hour is at hand and the Son of Man is betrayed into the hands of sinners." The Father had chosen the hour and the Son voluntarily submits Himself to even the most minute details — even the time schedule. God's plans moved flawlessly along.

For a moment it looked like Peter would ruin things. He had

tried this before when he attempted to dissuade Jesus from going to Jerusalem to His death. Now the overenthusiastic disciple pulls out his sword. Jesus rebukes him with the reminder that God's plans in the Old Testament take precedence over even the deepest loyalty. "But how then should the Scriptures be *fulfilled* that it *must* be so?" There was no way of getting around the inevitable.

This is not the place to show how many times the Old Testament is applied to Jesus in the New Testament. Many scholars have no use for what is called Messianic prophecies. They claim that the Old Testament prophets were just speaking to the people of their day and that their message was exhausted by contemporary events and persons. The reasons for their disbelief and weakness cannot be presented here. Rabbi Hugh Schonfeld in his widely publicized book, *The Passover Plot,* supports the idea that Jesus not only read the Old Testament but also tried to act out the Messianic role deliberately. Of course the rabbi holds that Jesus was somewhat of an imposter and that his scheming did not work.

Regardless of the glaring insufficiencies in the rabbi's position, it is an interesting testimony to the fact that God *did* lay down some definite plans in the Old Testament for the Messiah and that Jesus submitted Himself to them. Some scholars, who are really quite agnostic even about the existence of Jesus, offer the theory that Matthew, for example, wrote the account of Jesus' suffering with a copy of Psalm 22 and Isaiah 52 and 53 in front of him. Unlike these scholars, Christians have no hesitancy in asserting the real and historical existence of Jesus; but these scholars are right in pointing to the obvious parallels between these particular portions of the Old Testament and the account of Jesus' suffering.

Sometimes Christians call Jesus the Lord of Scriptures. At least from what we know about Jesus in the Gospels — and these are our best, earliest, and obviously only legitimate sources — He is the Servant of the Scriptures. This is not to deny that it was the Son of God who really was speaking to the Jews in the Old Testament, but in the New Testament He appears, as St. Paul says, in the form of a servant. Not even the Son of God in human form can escape the divine directives.

The Price

Everything and everyone in the world has his price. Some famous men have a speaking fee of several thousand dollars for an hour. Others will speak for nothing. The right amount of money in the right places often brings about the desired end. Kidnappers demanding ransoms and prison inmates holding guards as hostages are waiting for their prices to be met before releasing their victims. Jesus looked upon His life as a payment that had to be paid if man was to be released from sin and the fear of death.

The word for payment or ransom had many meanings for the Jewish people. The Lord God Himself had made the payment to release the Israelites from the hated Egyptian enslavement. God had looked upon the Jews as His own kinsmen or relatives and had offered His "outstretched arm" as the ransom price. The Jewish people had to buy their first-born boys back from God. God in turn regarded the Israelites as His first-born among all the families and nations of the earth. In this sense He bought them back not only from Egypt, but He rescued them from their iniquities and from the grave. He bought the Jews collectively as a nation for Himself and He acted individually in rescuing persons who demonstrated faith and repentance. The word for payment or ransom is also used to describe the animal or money that must be paid in the case of accidental death. The Jewish tradition is very rich in its understanding of payment or ransom. In Jesus God was making an adequate payment for the world's sins.

The Substitute

One of the Civil War practices which has since fallen into disuse was the use of mercenary substitutes. Men forced to serve in the army of the Union could and often did evade military service if they had the money to pay a substitute. Substitutes are simply parts of life. The stepfather or stepmother takes the place of the real parent. Catalogs of colleges and universities list

48

names of *acting* presidents, deans, and professors. During World War II the Germans invented a substitute coffee, and the Americans buttered their bread with margarine instead of the dairy product. Clergymen called vicars act instead of others. There is no need for further examples. A substitute is needed when the person or thing appointed to do the job cannot, for one reason or another, meet his obligations. The substitute assumes the responsibility for a task which he did not originally have.

Most pagan religions know of the concept of substitution. Human sacrifice meant death for some people in the religion community so that the remainder might be spared the wrath of angry deities. The Jewish people also knew the concept of substitution. They did engage at times in human sacrifice, but always at the displeasure of God. Genesis, the first book in the Bible, tells how Cain, Abel, Noah, Abraham, and others offered various sacrifices to God. Elaborate details for making commanded sacrifices can be found in the Book of Leviticus. The center of the worship life of the Jewish community was the Jerusalem temple with its altars crowded with animal sacrifices.

The Jewish sacrifice was a form of substitutionary payment for wrong which had been committed. Ingrained in the mind of the Jew was that for each sin God would extract a payment. The sacrifices never really did make adequate restitution to God, but they alerted the Jews to the justice of God. In addition to all the sacrifices, the high priest year after year on the Day of Atonement had to offer a sacrifice for all the sins of the people. For some sins no animal sacrifices could be substituted. If a life had been wrongfully taken, the life of the offender had to be taken.

Jesus understood His own life as substitution. He had come to earth not to receive the homage due God but to offer His life as a substitute payment in exchange for the life of the world. Behind this thinking that one Man, instead of sacrificial animals, would stand in the place of humankind, were certain key passages in Isaiah 53. The prophet speaks about a Servant who bears our sins and carries our iniquities. Not only does He bear the guilt of others, but the consequences of this guilt. Thus the Servant, not the people, is rejected by God.

Above it was said that a substitute is needed when the person originally given the task can no longer accomplish it, even if he wants to. Man by his own depravity and perverseness is so alienated from God that he is incapable of meeting God's requirements for him. The sad and pitiful thing is that man tries. Judas tried doing it with money and then his own life. Jesus had explicitly told His disciples there is nothing that a man can give to regain his life. This would have to be an action initiated and completed by God. He would provide the substitution. His name — Jesus.

The account of the trial and crucifixion is history, but it is more. Jesus is the "stand-in" for each man individually and for all mankind collectively. It is an account that cannot be read objectively, since the reader, no matter how disinterested and dispassionate, should really have been in Jesus' place.

The Life — The Blood

In many of the ancient mystery religions and modern cults, blood plays a prominent part in the worship ritual. To most people, with perhaps the exception of the clinically trained, the sight of blood causes deep feelings of repulsion, fear, and anxiety. The sight of blood suggests that a life has been violently taken or is at least threatened. It means that a person has not been allowed to finish his life in a normal way. Gruesome murder scenes and pictures of bloodied wounded men are photographically produced in color by only the most sanguine and sensational types of newspapers, magazines, and films. Good taste in our society makes every effort to cover up the traces of death taken in a violent manner.

The term blood also played a prominent role in the preaching of Jesus' apostles. Peter writes that we were ransomed or bought back not with gold or silver, but by the precious blood of Christ, who was like a lamb without imperfections. Of course at these words the Jew in the first century would immediately think about the sacrifice of lambs to atone for sins. The writer of the Book of Hebrews also states that Jesus has redeemed us through His own blood.

The Christian church has followed the direction of the apostles and has had a lot to say about blood in its hymns. One thinks about such well-known compositions as "Jesus, Thy Blood and Righteousness" and "Just as I Am Without One Plea But That Thy Blood Was Shed for Me."

All this "blood business" can be traced back to Jesus Himself. When He took the cup at the Last Supper, He initiated a blood theology with the words, "This is My blood of the covenant, which is poured out for many for the forgiveness of sins." What Jesus is saying is that His life offered in the violent manner of crucifixion would release people from their sins. Before Jesus' birth, Joseph had been informed of the redemptive characteristics of the Child. The concept of sin removal is not a new thought. Jesus adds the dimension of *His own* blood as the means for bringing this about.

As just stated, most men at the sight of blood surmise that life has come to a violent end. A natural death does not involve the shedding of blood. The Jewish people had an especially rich association with the whole concept of blood. Their existence as a nation from a loose confederation of families came about with their escape from Egypt in the exodus. They could not forget that on this occasion, while the eldest son in each Egyptian family was taken in death, the lives of their sons were spared. The lives of their oldest sons had been "bought" from the angel of death by the exchange of the lives of slaughtered lambs. Blood smeared on the front of Jewish homes was the signal to death's angel that God in His righteousness had been appeased by the blood of lambs. God would not extract the ultimate penalty of death from Jewish families. Just as the blood from thousands of lambs had been a declaration of independence for the Jews from their Egyptian captivity and which gave them a national existence, so the blood of Jesus poured out for the establishment of the covenant was creating the "new people of God."

Later in the prescribed sacrificial life of the Jews, blood would become the center of cultic attention. On the Day of Atonement, the high priest would first take the blood of the sacrificial goat and throw it in the direction of the altar, and then he sprinkled it upon the people. Such a ceremony would certainly strike most as being rather unusual. But there was no mystery in it for the Jew. Blood spilt on the altar signified that it would be only through death that God would be appeased. The remainder of the blood scattered on the Jewish people gathered for worship was the assurance that since God was now appeased, they would no longer have to fear His wrath. In the institution of the Lord's Supper, Jesus stands before His church as God's final High Priest. He pours out His own blood toward heaven and God, just as His predecessors had spilt the goat's blood on stone altars. Jesus' blood establishes the covenant with God. Then Jesus turns around and faces the universal church and offers His blood to His people, but now in a cup. When Christians participate in Christ's blood they know, just as the ancient Jews did, that their sins are forgiven because God has been appeased. In the new covenant God has gone a few steps further. The blood of brute animals has been replaced by the blood of God's own Son; and a superficial sprinkling is replaced by the much more intimate ritual of drinking.

In the Old Testament God had established the principle that wherever life was taken with premeditation another life had to be offered in exchange. On earth there is nothing more precious than the life of a man, since according to God's instructions to Noah, man is made in the image of God. Property can be destroyed and animals killed. These offenses can be rectified by a money payment. But no money can replace the life of a man. Judas had attempted this but without any success. Cain's curse is that as a marked man people throughout the world will recognize him as the first murderer. The lives of innocent men taken in vengeance murders demand restitution by taking the life of the offender. God tells Cain that the blood of Abel, his brother, is calling from the ground for vengeance.

This same type of blood restitution talk abounds throughout the rest of the Scriptures, but particularly in those few days just before the Crucifixion itself. In at least two cases Jesus informs the Jews that God is going to hold them responsible for the blood murder of the prophets. In the parable of the workers in the vineyard those who kill the servants and the son of the owner, that is, the prophets and Jesus Himself, must pay with their own lives. As Jesus says, "He will certainly kill those evil men." In a more explicit speech Jesus tells the Jews that they are responsible for the blood of all innocent men from Abel to Zechariah.

In addition to the words of Jesus during the last week about blood and blood guilt, there are a number of episodes during the same period of time that reinforce the thought that for death caused by vengeance, God in turn demands another death. The high priests refuse to take back the money from Judas which they had paid for the capture of Jesus because it is blood money, that is, money that has resulted in the death of a man who is innocent. Instead the money is used to buy a graveyard for paupers and strangers. The graveyard is called the Field of Blood since it was purchased with the money that was paid for the life of an innocent man.

Pontius Pilate stands before the Jewish crowd washing his hands in a gesture symbolizing with actions his words that he is not guilty of taking the life of a guiltless man. The Jews enthusiastically respond that Jesus' blood is upon them and their children, that is, they will gladly accept any responsibility for His death. From a historical point of view, the high priests, Judas, the Jewish crowds, and Pontius Pilate share equally and fully in the blood guilt of executing an innocent man. As any other murderers and their accomplices, they must expect to bear the consequences of their crimes. And they do.

The high priests and the Jews would lose the last vestiges of nationhood with the destruction of Jerusalem, their beloved capital city. Judas is doomed to suicide. Pontius Pilate, so secular sources inform us, would end his life in misery and failure. But here again we cannot let the historical details (let the reader understand this in the right sense) obscure the real action of the story. Of course God is interested that the guilty participants in this crime in the third decade of the first century A. D. pay. God is just in every case, even in the most minute, and seeks restitution. Still, a higher justice is being satisfied.

On that fateful Friday, God was not primarily concerned with the guilt of those whom history had happened to place on the scene. But on Calvary's hill God is making another Person pay —

and pay with His blood. God's justice is manifest in the death of public criminals. There can be no doubt about this. However, God's justice hovers over every man who has sinned publicly or in the hidden recesses of the heart. In God's eyes hate is on the same plateau as murder and eventually earns a murderer's penalty, death. Thus everyone must die. Now His prime concern was with the blood guilt heaped on the back of Jesus. So far as God was concerned, Jesus was the world's number one sinner. Not only His hands, but His entire body reeked of blood guilt and God was exacting the penalty, the blood of the offender.

If the reader is disturbed by these descriptions, let him remember the words of Jesus that He came to give His life as a ransom for many. Or, His blood poured out for many would be the basis of a new covenant. Since Jesus offered His life in blood, that is, violent death, I think we can understand why Christians have talked, sung, painted, and written so much about the blood of Jesus.

According to the Book of Revelation, the saints are washing their robes and making them white in the blood of the Lamb. One could quip here that this is God's own divine chemistry. It explains why Christians, especially at the time of crisis and death, receive Christ's blood in the cup. It was the blood that satisfied God's requirements. The details of the trial of Jesus and the death scenes themselves will further describe the shedding of blood.

Crucifixion – Sacrifice and Blood Offering

Isaiah, the Old Testament prophet, had already given the clue to the violent death that God's Servant would face at the hands of God Himself. He was to be smitten and afflicted by God. It was completely the planning of God that He should be beaten and whipped so that the soul or life of the Servant could be the offering for sin. God Himself had chosen the instruments of torture!

In the early church the disciples never simply proclaimed that Jesus had died, but that He died by crucifixion, that is, on a cross. References to the cross death are generously scattered in the New Testament. In a hymn that many scholars find to be one of the oldest in Christendom, Paul tells the Philippians that Jesus not only consented to humiliate Himself to the point of death, but even to death on a cross. In the first sermons of Peter to Jews in Jerusalem, he specifically mentions that they had put Jesus to death by a cross. Numerical counts at this time might be useless in demonstrating the obvious importance of the cross in the apostolic preaching. It can be pointed out, however, that in all the Gospels Christ's crucifixion is the high point and climax of the account. All of the events in each Gospel are on a line of ascension that points the reader's gaze to the cross. No other event or episode in the life of Jesus receives an even or near equal amount of attention to that of His death and the events directly leading up to it. His birth and resurrection (here we think of Christmas and Easter with their high celebrations in the church) do not even occupy the same amount of space in the Gospels — even when they are placed together.

Throughout His ministry Jesus was directing the gaze of His disciples to His final end on a cross. Christianity is not primarily the religion of Christ's incarnation or the resurrection, it is the religion of the crucifixion. What St. Paul said is still valid for the church: that he was determined to know nothing except Jesus Christ and Him crucified. Incarnation with nativity makes possible the crucifixion, and resurrection is crucifixion's divine certification. The beginning, heart, and end of Christianity is the crucifixion. The attention that our churches have given to the crucifixion through the adornment of our altars by crucifixes and the celebration of Lent is not at all amiss; it is putting the attention of the Christian where it should be — on the cross of Jesus. We must therefore understand carefully what crucifixion means.

According to all four Gospel accounts, the high priests acting in conjunction with the Sanhedrin find Jesus guilty of blasphemy. The evidence of the witnesses turns out to be inconclusive when contradictory testimony is given. The case is finally sealed against Jesus on the basis of His own admission in the form of an answer to a question that He was the Christ, the Son of God. According to a prescribed ritual, the ruling high priest, Caiaphas, tore his garment. This was a calculated action with feigned emotion. The usual penalty for crime of blasphemy was death by stoning, at least according to Leviticus 24:16. "he who blasphemes the name of the Lord shall be put to death; all the congregation shall stone him."

The Jews also knew of hanging as another form of execution. Hanging and crucifixion are similar. Crucifixion may be considered another form of hanging. The cross offered a more prolonged death than the quicker death by the rope. What type of death the Jews *really* preferred for Jesus is not known, but it is they and not Pilate who suggested crucifixion as the appropriate form of death for Jesus. Hanging implied the curse of God in a way that stoning didn't. According to Deuteronomy 21:22-23, the corpse of a hanged man is accursed by God and particularly offensive to Him. It defiles the land promised by God and given to the Jews as their own. In writing to the Galatians Paul is aware of theological significance of a death by crucifixion. "Christ redeemed us from the curse of the law, having become a curse for us—for it is written 'Cursed is everyone that *hangeth* on a tree.' " The unusually severe curse connected with hanging was its prolonged and excruciating form of death, in distinction from instant death. It symbolized the intense wrath of God over the particular form of sin which was receiving its just punishment.

In the light of the passage from Deuteronomy, St. Paul interpreted Jesus' death by hanging or crucifixion as an expression of God's curse. It was God who found that Jesus was accursed, "for a hanged man is accursed by God." Elsewhere in Matthew's Gospel there are the words of Jesus to the disciples to take up their crosses and follow Him. Jesus understands these crosses or afflictions of the disciples in the light of His own cross. The crosses for the disciples are not of their own choosing but of God's. Thus also *the cross* as an instrument of death is not Jesus' choice but a burden placed on Him by God to demonstrate that He was rejected and became repulsive.

Three Incidents: Scourging, Darkness, "Eli, Eli"

There is nothing in the Passion narrative which is not of im-

56

mediate redemptive significance. Three of these events need special attention—at least by a brief mention.

In Matthew's Gospel Pilate's order for crucifixion is given in the same breath as the one for scourging or whipping. As soon as the whips, knotted with small pieces of metal, struck the back of Jesus, God's redemptive process had moved into high gear. With each stroke the world's sin was being heaped upon Jesus; each time the burden became heavier. Isaiah had already said about 600 years before that "with His stripes we are healed." Peter reflecting on the same scene, the scourging of Jesus, would later say, "By His wounds you have been healed." What was physically detrimental to Jesus became spiritually beneficial to man.

Also in Matthew is the report of a darkness that blanketed the whole countryside for about 3 hours beginning about noon. It would not be adequate to state that the evangelist is merely informing his readers of local weather conditions in Palestine as available from the resident meteorologist. The significance of this darkness must be interpreted in the light of what the evangelists say about it in other places. The torture endured by the Son of God at the hands of an angry God cannot be understood by human minds and cannot be expressed in our words; but darkness will point us in the direction where the tragic drama is unfolded.

In addition to the reference to the darkness that covered the earth at the death of Jesus, Matthew uses the term darkness five times in his Gospel and each time the word has a religious or theological meaning and does not refer to phenomena in nature. In one place darkness refers to people living in sin and without hope and doomed to death (4:15-16). In the Sermon on the Mount it is applied to people who have deceived themselves into believing they are religious but still have not found the truth so far as God is concerned (6:23). In the other three places darkness means hell. The Jews, the original sons of the kingdom, are thrown into darkness because they refuse to accept their own Messiah. Their refusal is even the more hideous to God, since the Gentiles have recognized Him and are already sitting down with Abraham, Isaac, and Jacob at heaven's banquet (8:11).

The guest without the wedding garment, the imposter in the kingdom, is also headed for the "outer darkness." (22:13). The worthless servant who did not invest his own talent is doomed to the same fate (25:30).

In this one Gospel darkness suggests wrath, doom, ignorance of God, and hell, and throughout both Testaments these thoughts are connected with this word. In Joel and Zephaniah darkness carries with it the thought of the impending foreboding doom of God. In the New Testament Paul, Peter, John, and Jude all use it to describe that territory where Satan reigns. The darkness over the land of Palestine at the crucifixion of Jesus means that God was pouring down the wrath earned by His own people on the soul of Jesus. This wrath which Jesus had preached and warned about would find its target in His own soul.

A third incident in connection with the crucifixion has to do with a few foreign words. Our New Testament was written in Greek, but still here and there a few Hebrew or Aramaic words were left in the original even though they are written in the Greek alphabet. Where we find these foreign words in the text, we can conclude these words are old and important. The writer thought the words in the original language expressed a thought that could not adequately be translated into another language. Shortly before His death, Jesus uttered words that have been recorded in their original language and to which the evangelists give a translation. Jesus' words "Eli Eli, lema sabachthani?" (NEB) mean, "My God, My God, why did You forsake Me?" (Beck). In other places the Gospel writers have no hesitancy in translating any of the original preaching of Jesus into Greek, without giving the wording in the original, but these words expressed such a high and sacred mystery that they put them into their writings just as Jesus had spoken them.

One of the pictures of hell in the preaching of Jesus, as shown above, is dismissal from the presence of God. The servants in the vineyard who act murderously towards the king's servants and son are permanently exiled. Those who have not acted compassionately with the most insignificant follower of Jesus are told to depart. This is the judgment scene between the sheep and the goats. It is a parable of the final and last Judgment when Jesus seals the fate of the doomed with an irrevocable sentence, "Depart from Me!"

Just as the Son would order expulsion at the final eschatological judgment of the world, so now at the moment of crucifixion, the Father sits in the seat of judgment, faces the eternal Son, and utters the heavy judgment, "Depart from Me! You are accursed in My sight more than any man! The unrighteousness placed on You has made You an abomination in My sight!" From the defendant and victim comes the plea, "My God, My God, Why did You abandon Me?" (TEV)

The mystery of this moment is unmatched even by the other great mysteries: incarnation or resurrection. These words present a few questions. If the Father is God and Jesus is also God in the Trinitarian sense, how was it possible for God to forsake Jesus? What about the omnipresence of God? Isn't God present everywhere? Do the words of Jesus mean that the eternal Logos forsook Jesus as the Gnostics, an early heretical sect, taught. Where was the Spirit of God?

At this point a few distinctions can help us. The Trinity, the relationship between the Father, Son, and Spirit, is an eternal relationship. It existed before the created world and is not dependent upon anything that happens on earth, including the events in the life of Jesus. You might even say that the Son had a double role at that moment. He was both the punisher and the punished. (If you think of these things spatially, you will not understand.) The Trinity remained untouched even at this critical moment. God was also with Jesus as He is everywhere. He is even in hell, not to save but to sustain. Just as God would be with any condemned and dying man, He was with Jesus of Nazareth. Jesus was not excluded from God's omnipresence.

In addition, as a faithful child of God Jesus perceived God's special help. Jesus calls out not merely "God," but "My God." Still in another way the Spirit of God was also with Jesus because as God's representative Man, Jesus was given everything He needed to accomplish His task — even the Spirit. The writer of the Letter to the Hebrews even states that the eternal Spirit helped

59

Jesus make a sacrifice of His life to God. The separation of which Jesus cries from the cross is not a separation of the Trinity, not a separation from the sustaining presence of God, and not separation from the Spirit who never forsakes the faithful. It is the separation of the damned and condemned from God.

Who Is on the Cross?

In recent New Testament scholarship there has been a tendency to look askance at the church's doctrine of the Trinity which holds that one God is present in Three Persons, Father, Son, and Holy Spirit. Dependent on this doctrine is the doctrine of the incarnation which holds that the Son, the Second Person of the Trinity, became man in Jesus of Nazareth. Some have contended that these teachings came into existence in a later period of the church and that they reflect a strong Greek influence.

Regardless of these theories, Matthew's Gospel, which is the most Jewish of all the Gospels and perhaps the only one that was written in the Jews' native land and the homeland of Jesus Himself, has nine explicit references to Jesus as the Son of God. This one alone contains the phrase "Father and Son and Holy Spirit." What is even more revealing is that the phrase "the Son of God" is more frequently used in connection with His death than on any other occasion recorded in the Gospel. By actual count, Jesus is called the Son of God nine times in this Gospel of Matthew: twice by Satan in the temptation scenes, once by demons, once by Peter in the great confession, once by the disciples at the miraculous draught of fishes, and *four* times in connection with His death!

The high priest asks Jesus whether he is the Christ, the Son of God. To this question Jesus gives an affirmative answer. The mocking taunting crowds cluttered around the cross shout up to the tortured victim that if He is the Son of God He should make His own arrangements to come down. Again, they suggest that since *"He said* that He is the Son of God," He should be able to save Himself. The death scene concludes with the postscript from the centurion, "Truly this was the Son of God." Whatever else the evangelist wanted to teach in connection with Jesus' crucifixion, he most certainly wanted to teach that the victim on the cross is none other than the Son of God Himself. The blood sacrifice nailed to the cross was God Himself.

To this point the evangelist has painted a masterful picture. Jesus is not only the Son of God in faith or for faith, He is the Son of God (not the Redeemer in faith) also for those who do not benefit from His work. Satan, the demons, the high priest, and the Jewish crowds, wittingly or unwittingly, provide testimony that Jesus is the Son of God. Jesus Himself does not deny but affirms the allegation in the trial before the high priest. Even Peter and the disciples, who are sincere in their affirmations of Jesus' deity during the last week, are weak in commitment and somewhat deficient in their understanding.

The finale of the nine confessions is left not to a Jew, one of God's people, and not to a disciple, one of Jesus' people, but to a Roman centurion, a twice-hated man, a Gentile, and a subjugator of God's people. From him come the formal words of confession, "He really was the Son of God."

At death the remains of the deceased or the corpse must be recognized by the next of kin or a friend. This is a legal procedure. Some, like Joseph of Arimathea, come and claim the body; but only one is unhesitating about the true identity of the dead body. This is not merely the body of a rabbi or teacher of Nazareth. This is the body of the Son of God Himself!

As soon as we understand that God was the victim on the cross, all the rest of Jesus' life comes into focus. The angel had already informed Joseph that Mary's child would save His people from their sins — only God can do that. Jesus said that His life would be the ransom payment for the sins of the whole world — but is there a sufficient price in life or money that can make restitution for each and every sin? Can God in any way be satisfied? Who is able to meet God's requirements? Matthew's answer is that God Himself has provided an answer to the dilemma in Himself. What happened on the cross was really a private matter *in God*.

Paul would later write that God was in Christ reconciling the world to Himself. Matthew teaches the same thing. God was in heaven as the avenger of justice and He was on the cross as the victim of justice. Since the victim was the Son of God Himself, the victim's death had all the value and force of the death of God. It was as infinite in its scope as God Himself. It was the "supercosmic" event because the person dying could not, as Solomon said in his prayer at the dedication of Jerusalem's temple, be contained by an earthly building, or even earth or the highest heavens. At the death of God, the earth offered a minor salute with a tremor to recognize an event that was more than universal. Justice had placed the world's sin in the balances with the death of God, and it pronounced a verdict of innocence and righteousness over the world.

There are several places and circumstances in the Scriptures where Jesus can be seen clearly as Lord and God. He called the creation into existence and showed His creative control through His miracles. Today He still demonstrates His power in directing the course of history and of the nations for the benefit of His church. One day He will be acknowledged as Lord and God even by those who opposed Him and His cause on earth. But there is *one* place and only *one* place where He really desires recognition of Himself as Lord and God and that is on the cross. The cross with its agony is not separate from God, but in Jesus they have become one. The Christian religion is a theology of the cross.

Whoever is so offended by a God on the cross that he refuses to acknowledge the divine in the midst of that agony will be excluded from the final reign of Jesus. Peter had seen the miracles of Jesus and heard His preaching and confessed that Jesus was the Son of God. The Roman officer had heard the cries of the victim and seen the suffering and saw God's *real* work. And he saw *more* than Peter. Right on the cross God was *more* of what it really means to be God than in any other moment of history. (Let the reader understand this correctly!) Justice and love had met, neither was destroyed, but both were reinforced. The result was the agony of the Son of God Himself.

Matthew must have thought how difficult people would find the concept of a "God on a cross." On that account he brings down the curtain on Golgotha with not merely, "He was truly a righteous man," or even, "He was the Son of God"; but with "He was really God's Son." "Without a doubt, this Jesus was the Son of God" is another way of saying it. Let not the heavens and the earth be searched for God. He can be found on the cross.

Strange as it may sound the One on the cross was also the King.

CHAPTER V

King Jesus

God's Preparations for the King

In recent years many new churches have adopted the name for themselves "Christ the King." A very nice sounding name, the phrase is however redundant because "Christ" and "King" are synonymous to some extent. Since the time of Saul, the king in Israel was the "Christ," because he was inaugurated into the royal office with the pouring of oil. Each king in his own time had been chosen by God to be a redeemer in Israel, though they hardly lived up to these redemptive expectations in any sense. Still each king, regardless of his imperfections, was in himself a living prophecy of the final and even the eschatological Christ. As mentioned previously, Matthew begins his Gospel with a royal genealogy: 14 progenitors of kings, 14 kings, and 14 descendants of kings — all culminating in the most magnificent scion of the royal family, Jesus Himself. In another way "Christ" is more than just king. He is not only the king from the kingly family, but He is, as John says in the Book of Revelation, "the King of kings."

The early hope of Israel, at least according to the first parts of the Old Testament, was that through *one* man God would provide a solution for man's dilemma. Through the passing of years the focus of God's attention continued to narrow itself down: first a man, any man; then Noah, Shem, Abraham, Isaac, Jacob, and Judah. For nearly half a millennium, the situation was left there. The future expectations of the Jews for deliverance first focused down to a pinpoint light on the office of the king in Israel with a special statement of prophecy of Nathan to David. The Mosaic code had made preparations for a king, but God's ultimate deliverance of His people was attached to the royal office at that time by Nathan. Saul had been king, but in God's plans he would have nothing to do with God's ultimate Christ. This honor would belong to David.

A critical period in the history of the Jews had come to a near successful conclusion with the anointing of Saul. The nation had for many years lived as a loose confederation of tribes. Saul was established as king, but the tribes had reserved for themselves many of the basic political powers. When Saul faltered, David was chosen for the royal office; however, there were many obstacles that had to be surmounted before he could establish himself in his position. Saul's family still made a claim to the throne, even after his death. David's marriage to one of the daughters did not allay the claims of Saul's descendants. In addition many of the officers who had served with Saul could not easily switch their military allegiance to David, who had all the marks of an upstart and at times of a military insurgent. There were also the problems of the old tribal loyalties which Saul had encountered but had not overcome.

In capturing Jerusalem from the Jebusites, David had provided a center of attention for the nation. This would be the seat of royal power and the site of the temple. Now the national consciousness and the religious designs of the Israelites had one spot on which to focus their attention. The city of Jerusalem would serve as a unifying element for the Jewish people. [Now, 30 centuries later, it has not lost its power of attraction.] With the city captured, David could make plans for the palace and temple. It had looked like God's final kingdom was being ushered in with David. David had become a "Zionist." (Let the reader understand this correctly.) He wanted to actualize God's kingdom politically.

At that moment God intervenes and forbids David from going ahead with his 'millennialistic' plans. But when God takes away our fond hopes, he gives us better promises. David cannot build a house, that is, a building for God to live in, but David's house, his family, will rule forever. The words of Nathan, God's spokesman, "And your house and your kingdom shall be made sure forever before Me; your throne shall be established forever."

David is fully aware of what God has just done and praises

Him. Bethlehem's shepherd boy has become the "Shepherd of Israel" and this honor will belong to one of David's descendants in one way or another *forever*. God has now committed Himself — there is no turning back. Whatever God will ultimately do for His people will happen through David.

As David's gaze is directed far into the future, to the edges of eternity itself, God provides him with some information of immediate value. David's cherished dream of building the temple will be given to his immediate son, who, of course, is Solomon. Solomon, like David will be guilty of sin; however God will not desert him. Out of love God will chastise him so that in one way or another the Davidic line will be preserved in Israel. God's ultimate attention will not be on David's son Solomon, in spite of the great accomplishments of that king; it will be on the family or the *throne* of David. At least in four places both Nathan and David mention that David's throne is to last forever. Two prophecies are woven and twisted into one cloth: Solomon will fulfill David's political and religious aspirations for Jerusalem and Israel; and somehow the eternal aspirations of God for a people totally committed will also eventually come to completion.

The angel's message to Mary catches this line of reasoning in Luke's Gospel. "And the Lord God will give to Him the *throne* of His father David, and He will *reign* over the house of Jacob forever; and of His *kingdom* there shall be no end." Already in the time of David, the Jews caught the flavor of the prophecy. Psalm 45, a Messianic or royal Davidic psalm, speaks of David's throne like this: "Your divine throne endures forever." Hebrews 1:8 addresses these words specifically to Jesus, "Thy throne, O God, is for ever and ever." In David's throne God had made His futuristic redemptive plans Messianic or "royal" or even more specifically, "Davidic." The "Messianic ball" (let not the reader think this phrase irreverent) was tossed down the Davidic line from one king to another; but none, not even David, was able to fulfill the Davidic requirements. Solomon, David's son of promise, ended his royal career in disappointment. As each generation stepped into the Messianic spotlight, there was hardly any improvement. With the Babylonian Captivity, which Matthew marks as a division in the genealogy, the Davidic descendants are no longer kings. Zerubbabel is governor — and for the rest, they are political and religious unknowns. Still, as Israel plummets to the depths of misfortune and with it go the fortunes of the Davidic house and throne, the prophets in the midst of gloomy and dreadful proclamations of the Law perfect Israel's hope for a perfect "David," a "David" who would meet God's expectations.

Before we focus the Davidic expectations on Jesus, who is, as Matthew says, the Son of David, more must be said about the office of the king in Israel. In Israel, God was really *the* King. From the time that God chose Israel for Himself God was established as King. Israel's charter set down in the Books of Exodus and Deuteronomy, in particular, was in the language that a king sets down terms for a vassal lord. God's kingship over Israel was not abrogated when Saul assumed the throne or when kings were established over the Southern and Northern Kingdoms. The king in Israel was never absolute; he was really only God's representative. He was not king in his own right, but *the King's*, i. e., God's, representative. It was a constitutional monarchy with the king bound to the charter as put down in the Books of Moses. Therefore in regard to the northern kingdom, God continually disposed of the kings because they deliberately violated the Mosaic regulations. God was acting morally and in accord with the terms of the charter in bringing down kings and destroying the kingdom. Kings of the Davidic line in the South were hardly much better, but since God had made a promise to David, He had some ultimate or Messianic purposes to accomplish there. This promise did not prevent harsh pronouncements of the Law with appropriate punishments; but it did preserve the Davidic line.

Up to the time of Samuel, God ruled the Israelites directly through men chosen by Himself, called judges or deliverers. They helped God with special problems. When the problems disappeared, these men were no longer called upon to perform these functions. During the period of Samuel's leadership, Israel expressed a preference for a monarchy. Samuel quite naturally took this as a personal affront to his own leadership. God states that the greater affront is not to Samuel, but to God Himself.

The Israelites had separated themselves from God as their King. Saul would now have God's title, "king."

In the promise made to David in the next generation, the healing of the breach between God and the people begins. God does not abolish the throne in Israel. Instead He invests David's throne with the qualities of His own divine throne. David's throne in effect becomes God's throne, because only God's throne endures forever. Divine and human elements were joined together. In this way God was preparing His people for the incarnation of Jesus which would be the perfect union between God and man. The promises made to David made him a forerunner of the incarnation.

The word *king* for the Jewish people had a double intention: David and God. When the Davidic line was deposed politically from the throne, the Jewish desire for the ultimate Davidic king increased rather than abated. Through it all, the Jews still worshipped God as King. According to the Psalms, God was a great King above all gods and it was the duty of the pious Israelites to make a joyful noise before the King, the Lord. In the Sermon on the Mount, Jesus uses the royal imagery very effectively in His discourse on swearing. Heaven is the throne of God; earth His footstool; and Jerusalem is the city of the great King. The distance between the earthly Davidic king and God the King grows increasingly narrower in the Davidic line and successfully merges in Jesus, who is *King* because He is David's Son and God's Son.

Nazarene — A Strange Title

Matthew closes the birth and childhood narratives of Jesus with the account of the return to Nazareth and claims that this was done in fulfillment of the prophets' prediction that He would be called a *Nazarene*. Nazareth, though only the name of a small village, would become a very important word. This is the city where the Messiah grew up and spent most of His years. It was this city that would make a lasting impression on Him as no other city could. Here the Gospel would be rejected because a prophet is without honor in his own country. The phrase, "What good thing can come out of Nazareth," is a proverbial expression for expressing contempt for people from small towns. Jesus was condemned officially as "Jesus of Nazareth" and this word *Nazareth* would grace the cross on which the Lord of glory died: "Jesus of *Nazareth* King of the Jews." To this very day the letters abbreviating this phrase can be found on Christian crosses: "INRI."

No research has found a direct prophecy which indicates that the home of the Messiah would be Nazareth — at least not in so many words. Some have confused the word *Nazarene* with *Nazarite;* Samson and John the Baptist were Nazarites; but this interpretation is hardly correct. A Nazarite made vows to God and abstained from strong drink. This hardly applied to Jesus who was derisively called a winebibber because He was constantly found where people were refreshing themselves with a little alcohol. A favorite picture of the kingdom in the preaching of Jesus was a banquet — not a fitting illustration for a Nazarite.

What Matthew is doing in calling Jesus a Nazarene, because of His connection with the city of Nazareth, is playing a little word game in good Jewish style. The basic consonants for Nazareth are *nzr* which are also basic consonants for the Hebrew word for a green shoot, *nzr*. In being called a *Nazarene* because He is from the city of Nazareth, Jesus is also fulfilling several Old Testament prophecies that called Him the "root" or the "shoot." Isaiah says that in God's final days a green young tender branch is going to come to Jesse's royal family "tree." This is hardly a statement of a botanist on saplings. Just as David came from Jesse's family, so from this same family God would provide a new king. Now this time Jesse's family looked even less promising than when David was chosen. It is compared to a stump, the haunting reminder of a glorious past, but with little or no future. The prophet Jeremiah captures the same thought and says that God will raise up for David a "Branch" who will reign as King and bring redemption to Judah.

Nazarene combines the thoughts of royalty (the eschatological scion of the Davidic House) and humility (a king who is unheralded, unhonored and yes, even unrecognized.) The Root, the *nzr* was interpreted messianically in the Qumran community near the Dead Sea, where the Root sings in one of their hymns, "I thus became the despised." A medieval German hymn slightly adjusted the imagery of the branch to fit the cold Germanic winters of central Europe: "Behold, a Branch is growing Of loveliest form and grace, As prophets sung, foreknowing; It springs from Jesse's race And bears one little Flower In midst of coldest winter, At deepest midnight hour." God is the King, but He acts royally in the most unconventional ways and in the most unexpected places — Nazareth. If Nazareth is astonishingly "the seat of royal power," how much more unfitting will be the throne on the cross.

Who is the Son of David? Solomon or Jesus

Throughout the Gospels, Jesus is referred to as the Son of David. In some cases the believing Jews address Him with this designation, a very fitting title for the final and eschatological Davidic king. Son of David is simply another way of saying Christ or King. All of these thoughts were brought together in Psalm 2. In this psalm God looks favorably upon the Davidic descendant. It is the Lord who sets David's Son on David's throne and anoints Him; that is, God makes Him the Christ.

In the genealogy in Matthew, Jesus is specifically called the Son of David. The blind men who call out for help use these same words as a form of address. In the section where Jesus is accused of driving out devils with the help of the devil, Jesus is referred to first as Son of David by the admiring crowds who ask, "Can this be the Son of David?" On Palm Sunday additional crowds of admirers sing "Hosanna to the Son of David." In the final week Jesus puts to the religious leaders a theological question about the identification of the Son of David on the basis of Psalm 110. "How can David's Son be David's Lord?" There is no reason to doubt the tradition that David spoke these words, especially since it is endorsed by Jesus. It is quoted in all three synoptic Gospels, and all assign the words directly to David.

Whom David was addressing in this psalm is another problem. The problem begins to evaporate when we take this section in connection with the promise of Nathan to David that His throne would be an eternal one and with Psalm 2 where God makes the Davidic king not only the Christ, i. e., the Anointed, but also His Son.

The occasion for these words could have been the last days of David when a quarrel arose among David's sons over the succession to the crown. The first two chapters of 1 Kings describe the struggles. The question was through which son of David would God act *messianically* to redeem His people. Just as God had focused His Messianic attention on David, so this attention is directed by David to Solomon. Nathan the prophet had directed David to do this.

The Messiah would not only be Davidic, He would be Solomonic. The Solomonic Messiah would not only possess David's regal qualities, but like Solomon He would become a priest for His people. On this account David describes the Solomonic Messiah as being a successor also of Melchizedek, who as the priest-king had ruled Jerusalem a millenium before. Psalm 110 embodies temporarily the Messianic hope in Solomon, just as Nathan's words had focused this hope in David a generation before. Jesus was aware that He was not only the Davidic king but the Solomonic priest-king. Jesus also stands in the succession of priest-king Melchizedek, the king of righteousness, who was also king of Salem, that is, the king of peace.

In the Sermon on the Mount Jesus says that the splendor of Israel's most illustrious king, Solomon, in no way compares with God's work in nature. How much more splendid must the Creator Himself be! Jesus! In still another place Jesus speaks about the queen of the South who came "halfway round the world" to hear the wisdom of Solomon. In Jesus *Someone* greater than Solomon is present. The splendor and wisdom of Solomon had no earthly competitors, yet they were imperfect in comparison to Jesus who was perfect in these respects. David had looked messianically upon Solomon, who first was a "son of promise" then a "son of disappointment." In Jesus David's fondest dreams now had come true.

There are other allusions to Jesus as the full embodiment of the anticipated Solomonic glory. The parables of Jesus dealing with the themes of the bridegroom, the bride, the wedding, and the marriage reflect the beautiful love themes from the Song of Solomon. Jesus is the King's Son who takes the church as His bride.

In Israel, the *true* king was a son of God and a son of David. At first there had been hope that Solomon might be *that* son in perfection, but as a patron of idolatry within His own home he became in fact a prodigal son, a true son of dust in turning away from the Creator-Father to the productions of his own imagination. Solomon, whose name means PEACE, sowed the seeds for war and the internal destruction of God's nation, Israel. The Jews looked back with nostalgia on what Solomon might have been but was not. Only if David's faithfulness and Solomon's glory could be found in one Man! Isaiah portrayed the birth of the ultimate Solomonic king when he spoke of the birth of the "Prince of Peace." Angels caught the drift of it all in singing at the birth of the Solomonic king, "Glory to God in the highest and on earth *peace*." Jesus was that *Solomon*, the man who makes peace between God and man, David's true Son, the expected Solomon. It is not surprising that the Gentile Magi paid homage to Jesus, the Davidic Jewish King, just as the Gentile monarch of Sheba had come to see Solomon, who was also God's king.

One other event in the life of Jesus had definite Solomonic overtones. Jesus' entry into Jerusalem upon a donkey must have reminded the Jews of the account where Solomon is proclaimed by David to be the king. In order to settle the problem of the royal succession, David had Solomon sit on the royal mule and ride through the environs of Jerusalem so that the people could hail him as king. The Jews of course did not find in Solomon God's final king. Zechariah, the prophet, spoke of another King who would come riding on a donkey. On that Palm Sunday morning, the heart of the Jewish populace went out to meet God's final Solomon.

Something Greater than the Temple:
Another Allusion to Solomon

Matthew, more than the other Gospel writers, likes to play

around with the concept of the king. Kingship and kingdom really meant a lot to the Jews. Throughout his work, the Evangelist drops some not-so-gentle hints to the royal personage of Jesus. Some of these have already been indicated: the Davidic genealogy, David's Son, the references to Solomon, and the parables with the wedding imagery. There are in addition some direct references to Jesus as the King.

The Magi from the East show up in Herod the Great's court in Jerusalem, asking where they can find the recently born "king of the Jews." Here is a situation with a little divine humor. According to Matthew, the first ones who come looking for the Jewish king are Gentiles! What an indictment this must have been against Jews and the Jewish-Christians in and around Jerusalem at the time when Matthew wrote his Gospel. Matthew develops this theme right through to the end of the Gospel. Consider the Roman centurion, the Syrophoenician woman, and the centurion at the cross — all Gentiles.

Second, Matthew never calls Herod the "king of the Jews," this title is reserved for Jesus. To be sure, Herod had the title of "king of the Jews" but it was given by the Romans and he himself was an Edomite and not a Jew. For political expediency he had adopted the Jewish faith, but he also became a patron of Roman temples and constructed Roman type baths and athletic stadiums — all abominations to the Jews. Herod was not unlike his Jewish predecessors in Jerusalem and Samaria, 600 to 900 years before, who gave political and financial support to paganism. The Jews living in the middle of the first century in Jerusalem had no use for Jesus as their king, but Herod, a living reminder of the apostate kings in Jewish history, was hardly a better choice!

The only other time outside of the birth narratives where the term king is specifically used of Jesus is during the final week of His life. In the parable of the sheep and the goats, Jesus, using His usual self-designation Son of Man, says that the King shall make the final Judgment between the redeemed and the damned. The term King is like that of the Son of God in Matthew in that both phrases are most frequently used in connection with actual suffering of Jesus. He is asked by Pilate whether He is really the King of the Jews. During the mocking, the soldiers greet Him with the words, "Hail, King of the Jews." The inscription above the cross reads, "Jesus of Nazareth *King* of the Jews." (That information is so important that all four Gospel writers contain it in one form or another.) A final cacophony is provided by the Jewish crowd on Golgatha. "He saved others; He cannot save Himself. He is the King of Israel."

Before we said that God was *really* God on the cross; now we can say again that the one place where Jesus is *really* King is on the cross. Jesus is the King whom the Magi worship and the King who makes the final eschatological judgment, but He is also the King who is tried and sentenced by Pilate, mocked by soldiers, jeered by Jews, and heralded by the royal writ above His thorn encircled head, INRI: Jesus of Nazareth King of the Jews.

The cross was the only fitting place for the true King of the Jews to be. The Jews understood the royal obligation and predicament correctly when they made fun of Him with the words: "He saved others; He cannot save Himself. He is the King of Israel." In the Old Testament it was God as the King of Israel who had redeemed and bought back His people. The kings of Israel were to perform this same function as God's representatives in protecting God's people and rescuing them when threatened. The reader does not have to be told that they were miserable failures in performing this function. Ten of the tribes disappeared, and the others were taken to Babylon to lose their national independence. Now Jesus, the final King of Israel as Son of God and Son of David was saving others, just as the Jews who were responsible for His death, had claimed for Him. He Himself was at that moment beyond redemption. (Let the reader understand this correctly.)

David had established this royal capital at Jerusalem; and Jesus had prohibited oaths taken by Jerusalem because it is the city of the great King, God. Still the Jews did not speak of two kings — God and David — both ruling in the same place. On Golgotha Jesus was establishing His royal capital. In Jesus both David and God were ruling as one King — from the same throne, a cross. Read through the Passion history according to Matthew again, and you will see that the phrases *king* and *Son of God* each are here more frequently used of Jesus than in any other part of that Gospel. Maybe Matthew is trying to tell us something. The cross has become the divine throne.

One King or Two? A Few Trinitarian Thoughts

In the discourses of the final week, Jesus uses the title king both of Himself and of His Father. In the parable of the king's son where the king prepares a wedding feast for his son, the king is Father and the son is Jesus, that is, God's Son. However in the parable of the sheep and the goats, the king is Jesus Himself. Does this mean that Jesus distinguished His reign or kingship from that of the Father? The relationship between Solomon and David could give us a few answers. At least in the case of Solomon he was proclaimed and recognized as king before his father, David, died. The First Book of Kings does not tell us the length of time between the proclamation of Solomon and the death of David; however, in that period both were called king, King David and King Solomon. Both shared one throne and ruled one kingdom without any political animosity. The kingdom of this father and this son was one. Solomon was expected to follow in his father's footsteps. This resembled Jesus and His Father, who are both called King and who both share in the same tasks because of their essential unity. In the parable of the king's son, it is the father as king who brings judgment upon the murderers of the servants and his own son; and in the parable of the sheep and the goats it is the son as king who makes the final eschatological judgment. As history informs us, Solomon was not really a son after David's heart. The Book of 1 Kings contains the mournful lament that Solomon's heart was not perfect as was the heart of David, his father. With Jesus, God found a Son who lived up to all His expectations; His heart was like David's in relying only on the Father's mercy. In Jesus, Father and Son are of one mind.

Now what was (is) the nature of His Kingdom?

CHAPTER VI

The King and His Kingdom

Israel as a Kingdom

The plans for a kingdom were already set down in the Book of Deuteronomy by Moses. In the reigns of David and Solomon, Israel reached the pinnacle of religious and political greatness. Never again in later history would political greatness be matched by such religious fervor. After Solomon the kingdom was divided into two parts: Israel was the name for the northern part and Judah for the southern. In spite of spurts of political and religious vigor in each kingdom, both headed down the road to idolatry with the north somewhat outpacing the south.

Israel completely lost its national identity, and Judah even after a release from captivity did not regain its national independence. In the five hundred or so years before Christ, the returned captives would have many problems, but idolatry would not be the major one. With the exception of about one hundred years, the kingdom was not restored during this period. Even during these times, the influence of neighboring nations played a large role in the internal politics of the Jews.

In spite of all the humiliation which the Jews had experienced over the centuries, the thoughts of the restoration of the kingdom stirred the heart of every patriotic Jew. When John the Baptizer and Jesus began their ministries preaching the coming of God's kingdom and its nearness, it received immediate reception, but there was hardly any unanimity on what this meant to the hearers. For some it meant the restoration of David's political kingdom, adorned by the glories of Solomon. In the immediate context of that time it certainly included the overthrow of the forces of occupation of Caesar's empire, who marched under the hated symbol of the Roman eagle. For others the kingdom was chiefly religious but not less Davidic. After the time of David this king was held up by the writers of the Old Testament as an example of a man whose heart really belonged to God. Politically he was successful and great, and he never was so stiffnecked and hardened in heart as not to acknowledge his sin and to repent of it publicly. It seems that very, very few of the Jews looked for this kind of kingdom, centering in repentance and forgiveness.

Simeon, who greets the 40-day-old Christ Child in the temple, is pictured as one who is waiting for the redemption of Israel. He understood the kingdom in this kind of religious sense. The redemption he looked for was of such a kind that he could peacefully die since his offenses had already been covered by God. It was this kingdom, a kingdom that centered in making people right with God, that Jesus brought with Him.

Both the Jews and Jesus wanted to restore David's kingdom —but in different senses. To most of the Jews in Jesus' day, David was great because of his political exploits. To Jesus David was great because he acknowledged his offenses against God and was enveloped by God's grace. Yes, Jesus was continuing the kingdom of David, but it was not the kingdom that the politically oriented Jews wanted.

The kingdom God was bringing centered in Jesus and His redemptive work. He became truly God's king on the cross. The subjects of this kingdom were those who accepted not only Jesus but also His work.

Unlikely Subjects

The kingdom of God breaks into the New Testament period with the preaching of God's wrath by John the Baptizer. Its message is that political connection to the kingdom hardly meets the requirements for kingdom membership. Without a complete internal reorientation of the heart to God, the kingdom will be taken away from the Jews. The biggest mistake is to consider the kingdom a permanent possession because of an unalterable decree of God. God's hands are never so tied to His own promises that He has to transgress His own righteousness. In the past He had taken the kingdom away from Israel in spite of the pitiful bleeding of His own heart. Nevertheless, those who do not meet kingdom requirements, regardless of their political connections, are dismissed.

The Gospel account in Matthew is the story of how the Jews are being ripped off the tree, branch by branch, and being replaced by Gentiles. Right after Jesus had cured the centurion's servant and remarked on the greatness of the centurion's faith, Matthew records this verdict of Jesus that those who belong to the kingdom, that is, the Jews, are being thrown into darkness, while the Gentiles are eating at the same table with the three patriarchal greats: Abraham, Isaac, and Jacob. How offensive this must have been for good Jewish ears! If Jesus was censured for eating with outright sinners and publicans, people nevertheless with good Jewish blood, how grotesque to state that Gentiles could make it up to the head table. These were words of ancestral sacrilege.

But it is right here that we see the true mark of the kingdom: it includes people who do not really belong there. Or, to use the phrase of Hosea, people who are *not* the people of God have become His very own people. This is what grace really means.

The genealogy in Matthew prepares the self-righteously religious reader for the type of people Jesus intends to put in His kingdom. There's the blue-ribbon list that would make it into any religious 'who's who': Abraham, Isaac, Jacob, Judah, David, Hezekiah, and Josiah. The surprise comes with the listing of three adulteresses: Tamar, Rahab, and Bathsheba, whom Matthew calls with a little contemptuous humor "Uriah's wife." This is striking the self-righteous people where it hurts. The other surprise is the listing of Gentiles: Rahab and Ruth. This was just a small Gentile stream in the Old Testament, but with the coming of Jesus, first-class sinners and Gentiles, people not chosen by God, were now being chosen by Him.

The truly "greats" in the kingdom are not Jews, but the Gentile Roman centurion and the Caananite woman. And marching into the kingdom before the religious temple teaching authorities are the tax collectors and prostitutes. There are some people whom God really wanted to include in His kingdom, but who when the chips were down refused to come. Some of Jesus' kingly ancestors were not only run-of-the-mill unbelievers, but they directly opposed the God of Israel by setting up idols and endorsing, with financial and political support, false religions. Abijam, Ahaz, and Manasseh are cases in point.

Many of Jesus' parables developed this line of thinking. The parable of the workers in the vineyard and one about the wedding of the king's son teach among other things that those for whom the kingdom was originally intended are now excluded because of their own choice. They not only refuse God's invitation to believe, but they do everything in their power to hinder the work of God's servants.

Since the Jews have refused membership in His kingdom, God includes those who were not really destined at first to become members. Men prominent because of wealth and position squeeze into the kingdom only under the greatest amount of effort. Children, who always play an inconsequential role in society because they are recipients of culture rather its creators, are held up as outstanding examples of those who can hold kingdom membership. Those who set their minds on having the most prominent places in the kingdom are relegated to positions of relative unimportance; and those who serve the kingdom without thought of reward take the seats of honor. Teachers who disregard the king's orders barely get in, if they get in at all. Kingdom membership is not earned, "but it is for those for whom it has been prepared by (Jesus') Father."

The old kingdom of Israel relied heavily on blood relationship to Abraham; the new kingdom places total value on an individual's faith. Who really is in the kingdom is hidden to human observation. All Christians are given the warning not to make any judgments concerning anyone else besides the customary judgments on the basis of confessions of faith and of blatant offenses against God's moral law. The kingdom is never the home of those who deny the King and His edicts. Only God sees into the hearts of men, and angels will carry out for Him the final division; therefore the church's judgment in one sense is necessarily superficial.

This really is not here an advancement over the older type kingdom in Israel. The political kingdom or nation of Israel was God's chosen vehicle where the true Israel was hidden. It was God's chosen shell to protect those who were really faithful; but still it was only a shell. This is what St. Paul means when he says that all Israel, that is, the nation, is *not* Israel, that is, God's elect.

Since the time of Christ, the established church is the shield under which God protects His kingdom. It is not only wrong but also dangerous to identify and make a one-for-one identification between the established church and the kingdom. God's kingdom is found no place except inside the church walls where the Gospel of Jesus is preached and His sacraments are administered; still the kingdom is not, in so many words, the established church. The kingdom is hidden and appears unpretentious. Its beginnings are always inconsequential, but its final and last stage of development is magnificent.

Scattered through the church along with the kingdom members are the members of Satan's kingdom. They are always more industrious, illustrious, and seemingly more intelligent than the children of light. Satan's allies are always working from within and attacking the kingdom. Jesus spoke about this in stating that the kingdom of heaven continually endures violence. Through God's continued direction of the kingdom, it survives under the most oppressive conditions. Grace, and grace alone, holds the kingdom together and keeps it going. This is what the kingdom *of God* means. Its origin is in heaven not on earth.

If God upholds the kingdom by grace, faith is the only proper response of the kingdom members. An entire host of unlikely candidates meet this requirement: the Canaanite woman, the Roman centurion, the children brought to Jesus, the dying thief, and the Roman centurion at the cross. Impostors try to get into this kingdom without this requirement and have no intention of meeting it. Thus the wedding guest was thrown into the outer darkness because he did not wear the wedding garment, faith. Wherever the Word of God, which centers in the death and resurrection of Jesus, is preached there God's kingdom is establish-

ing beachheads in the world. This is the kingdom's only weapon —
at least according to Jesus and St. Paul.

Still Another Kingdom

It is proper to say that the kingdom is going through stages
of development, at least in a certain sense. The political prominence of the Davidic kingdom pointed to the spiritual prominence
of Jesus' kingdom. This kingdom is now among us with the
preaching of the Word. This aspect of the kingdom will give way
to still another. Today the kingdom is in the stage of humiliation;
but the day is coming when this kingdom will shine with God's
own glory. Especially during the final week of Jesus' life, He
spoke of Himself coming from heaven as the final judge of the
world to reward both the good and the evil. He even told the high
priest, Caiaphas, that He would come on the right hand of power.
Unlike the present kingdom, which is hidden to the eye of un-
belief, the final revelation of the kingdom will escape no one's
purview. It will not come under the signs of the humiliation of
preaching and the sacraments, but it will break in from the outside. All the world will know it, and it will be the first universal
or cosmic observable revelatory event since the great flood. This,
by the way, is an analogy which St. Peter makes. The kingdom
members within the church pray that God will soon reveal His
kingdom in glory, but those who belong to Jesus can never forget
that all aspects of the kingdom are by grace. Just as God chooses
where and when kingdom preaching shall take place, so God de-
cides when the kingdom shall break through in glory. The church
has no right or authority to bring about the glorification of the
kingdom on earth. This is a theology of glory as opposed to a theology of the cross. God and not man will glorify the church. To do
or act otherwise would be to destroy the principle that everything is by God's grace alone.

An Absolute Kingdom

The kingdom which comes by preaching is one of humiliation and can be rejected. The kingdom that breaks through from

heaven comes with power, might, and glory; but this kingdom still lies somewhere in the future. It is not here. There is still another aspect of God's kingdom, if we dare call it that, which works without fail and with total power right now. All things, and here the dimensions are cosmic and universal, are under Jesus' direct supervision and direction. Outside the church, Jesus as God's representative in the world directs all natural events and political actions for the ultimate good of the church. When Pilate threatened Jesus with the political power of the Roman Empire, Jesus responded that Pilate would have no power without the consent of heaven. Paul in Colossians speaks about Jesus holding things in the world together.

The last verses of Matthew's Gospel picture Jesus standing as the cosmic man and the new Adam who will exercise a total dominion over heaven and earth. He states with clarity that *all* power or authority is given Him in heaven and earth. Jesus here is speaking as *a* man and not as God. His God-authority as Creator He always had and He did not receive it from anyone. Yet He says that authority is given Him, but it is the cosmic authority which is given to Jesus as the Christ, as the truly ideal man. For Jesus to be the Christ or the Messiah means that He is the representative Israel, or still better, the representative Davidic king. Now with these words, "All power is given to Me," Jesus steps forward as the primeval man. His words recall Psalm 8: "What is man that Thou art mindful of him, and the Son of Man that Thou dost care for Him? Yet Thou hast made Him a little less than God, and dost crown Him with glory and honor. Thou hast given dominion over the works of Thy hands; thou hast put all things under His feet." Here is the picture of man in the original state of perfection, a condition now lost. Adam and his progeny should have lived up to this graphic description of men in the perfect relationship with God, but they did not and could not. Jesus sees the obligations and fulfills them for all perfectly. He is all what Adam originally was and even more. As the new Adam and the representative of the human race, He earns back the authority which we once lost. As the truly representative man Jesus is God's vice-regent over the world. The Letter to the Hebrews draws out this picture of Jesus' cosmic dominion with even greater detail.

Some Kingdom Pitfalls

The church must be very careful to identify her task of preaching that kingdom which is now hidden beneath the earthly forms of the words and the sacramental signs. If she confuses her role and claims for herself an aspect of God's kingdom which God has not given her specifically, she no longer is God's servant and she brings disaster upon those whom God has entrusted to her care. The kingdom can be taken away from the church as punishment.

The most common error that troubles the church is that she somehow attaches to herself aspects of God's absolute kingdom and rule in nature and especially in politics. When God operates here, He operates with absolute sovereignty and tolerates no affront to His authority. Asserting that death and taxes are the two things of which there can be absolute certainty acknowledges God's complete control in nature and in the government. Unfortunately the church sees herself frequently as wielders of this type of absolute authority. Even Jesus' disciples looked upon the kingdom politically. When Jesus had risen from the dead, they even at that time asked Him about the political restoration of Israel. Of course even before He died questions of their political prominence often troubled them.

In the Middle Ages bishops and priests often exerted political power, which reached its acme in the pope. There is no age or century in which the church has not tried to make alliances with the state for self-protection and the propagation of the faith. Where the church relies on the absolute authority of God's absolute kingdom, her mission is truncated because she has tried to shed her marks of humility—a humility which was the mark of her Lord.

If the pope has represented an unfortunate merger of religious and political power in the Catholic Church, milliennialism represents a parallel phenomenon in the Protestant churches. Many fundamentalist Protestants are looking now to the modern state of Israel as the fulfillment of God's promises to the church. Somehow, it is believed, God will be vindicated ultimately in the political victories of this nation. Less fundamentalist Protestants are also somewhat "millennialistic" when they see the church as another political structure which can use its political clout to accomplish certain humanitarian ends. In this approach the church becomes simply another interest group in the game of power politics. This position has even gone to the extreme of advocating the overthrow of the established governmental structures, since, as it is argued, God is as much at work in the world as He is in the church. Such a concept overlooks the fact that even though God works in both the world and the church, He does something entirely different in each, and He does it in a different way. He is in the world to exert power and to restrain manifest evil. In the church God is present to proclaim forgiveness in Jesus' name.

There is no way of guaranteeing that the church will always do the kingdom work. A history of the church shows results quite to the contrary. Still the church can guard against these dangers when she realizes that she is on earth the home of that kingdom of God which is present only in the preaching of Jesus.

The King of this special kingdom has an extraordinary name.

CHAPTER VII

The Son of Man:
Another Strange Title

Of the many names and titles that have been used for Jesus none have presented as many difficulties as the phrase, the Son of Man. The meanings of Christ, Son of God, Savior, and Lord are much easier to determine. Most of the mainline Christian denominations have understood the phrase as referring to the humanity of Jesus in distinction to His divinity. A good example of this is the well-known hymn, "Beautiful Savior," where the Redeemer is worshipped as "Son of God and Son of Man." The use of the phrases in this way indicates that perhaps Son of God describes one aspect of Jesus' personality and the Son of Man another.

There are some obvious peculiarities about the phrase Son of Man. First of all, it is never found in any of the epistles, those sections of the New Testament Scriptures dealing with doctrinal and ethical problems in the early Christian congregations. The only place where it is used outside of the Gospels is by Stephen in Acts at the occasion of his martyrdom. "I see heaven opened and the Son of Man standing at the right hand of God!"

Second, in the Gospels the phrase is only found in the mouth of Jesus as referring to Himself. In these cases it is simply a synonym for the personal pronoun "I." There are some who hold that when the man Jesus spoke about the Son of Man, He was referring to an apocalyptic figure, a type of idealized glorified man, who would come streaming out of the heavens to save Him. Such a theory goes on to state that later the early Christian congregations made it appear as if Jesus were referring to Himself. Of course these assumptions are without evidence — in spite of the impressive scholarly credentials of those who hold these views. This theory holds that Jesus believed in a mythological figure called the Son of Man and that the early Christian congregations or literary editors so tampered with the wording that the original sense of the words were changed that Jesus appears as the Son of Man. Jesus would simply have been a misguided religionist susceptible to the belief in a fictitious Son of Man, and the early Christians would be guilty of what we would today call literary misidentification. Should either or both be the case, the Christian religion for this writer would have no interest — with perhaps the exception of the attention given to any ancient religious oddity.

Third, the phrase Son of Man is never used as a form of address. None of the disciples ever address Jesus as the Son of Man. There is not one instance recorded where the phrase is found in their mouths.

Fourth, the phrase Son of Man may be used as a synonym for I, but only in certain cases. It is used by Jesus in a definitely Messianic sense, that is, when He thinks about the obligations which God has placed upon Him.

Fifth, it is not used by Jesus after the resurrection.

Some scholars, and I think that they are right, can see three categories into which these obligations can be placed. (1) Jesus first of all uses the phrase of Himself to describe His authority exercised among men. It is the Son of Man who has authority on earth to forgive sin and who is the Lord of the Sabbath. (2) In those sections describing the end of the world (these are called apocalyptic because they are hidden and still not revealed as events to us), it is the Son of Man who makes the final Judgment. He sits as King and sends forth His angels to bring all men before the throne for the verdict. The Son of Man has universal jurisdiction. This goes back to an apocalyptic vision found in the Book of Daniel. (3) Jesus uses the phrase as He contemplates the crucifixion and its benefits. It is the Son of Man who gives His life as a ransom for many, and it is the Son of Man who goes as it is written of Him and who is arrested, crucified, and risen from the dead on the third day.

This strange title does not alone refer to the humanity of Jesus but also to the deity of Jesus during the period when He identified in a very real sense with fallen humanity. In strictly dogmatic language this is called the humiliation of Jesus. It embraces what the Nicene Creed calls "He was made man." In reciting the Creed some Christians genuflect at this point. It includes all the events in His earthly life, including the burial. In Philippians 2 Paul speaks about this period in Jesus' life, where he states that even though Jesus had everything that belonged to God, He refrained from open use of His powers, even to the point of experiencing a criminal's death by crucifixion. In short, Jesus uses the phrase Son of Man as a self-designation when He contemplates what He *as God* is enduring and will endure for the fallen race of men.

The Son of Man appears as an ordinary man among men, and in spite of obvious appearances He can forgive sin and regulate the Sabbath just as confidently as He can where His glory is evident and explicit. His assumed humanity has not encroached upon His God powers, which were evidently His before "He was made man." His right to judge the world and to hold sinners accountable has not been lost, even though for the sake of justice He must be judged and condemned by the Jews (the high priests and the Sanhedrin) and the Gentiles (Pontius Pilate). The person who puts His life in the balances of justice so that it can be a ransom for many is God Himself. Many had gone to Jerusalem for crucifixion, but it is only the Son of Man, God Himself, who would go there to redeem the world and on the third day rise again.

In the Old Testament the unique name of God which was revealed to the Jews through Moses was *Yahweh*, which is sometimes rendered in English as Jehovah. Through the passing of time the Jews regarded this name as so holy that they gradually refrained from using this name altogether. When they saw the name *Yahweh* in the sacred text, they made a substitution with one of the other names by which God was called. This was the name that God had chosen for Himself, and unlike other names it was not used of other gods.

In the New Testament it appears as if the disciples and the early Christians saw a similar type of sacred intent in the name for Jesus, Son of Man. Jesus was addressed as Son of God, the Son of David, Lord, and Christ, but He was never called the Son of Man. The other names had a note of triumph. In the final glorification the saints and angels praise Jesus as "the King of kings, the Lord of lords." But the phrase Son of Man has a note of sadness. It is God in human form who has to face the inevitable consequences of a fallen race. This was a task that had to be done and had a divine "must" written over it, but it was not a particularly happy or joyous task. The church could not forget that the Son of Man prayed the Father to remove the cup of wrath. This was real suffering — not a masquerade. *Yahweh* was the God who had chosen Israel as His own possession. The Son of Man was the God who not only chose Israel and the Gentiles as His own possessions, but who paid for the world with His own life given into death by crucifixion.

There are two passages in particular that clinch the argument that the phrase the Son of Man is Jesus' own designation for Himself as the Son of God in the self-assumed state of humiliation. When Jesus asked the disciples for a statement of commitment and confession concerning Himself, He addressed the question to them in these words, "Who do men say that I, the Son of Man, am."

The famous answer from Peter was that Jesus was the Christ, the Son of the living God. This pericope is parallel to the question from the high priest to Jesus about His being the Christ, the Son of God. After Jesus answers affirmatively, He goes on to speak about Himself as Son of Man who will come on heaven's clouds in judgment. The words are the same in both cases, but they are in reversed order. Son of Man is the Son of God, as asserted by Peter; and the Son of God is the Son of Man, as asserted by Jesus. Both assertions are replies to questions.

After the resurrection, Jesus does not use the term Son of Man again. The work of redemption and hence the necessity for humiliation are behind Him. He has completed the Messianic task. For this God has "highly exalted Him." The need for refraining from divine manifestation is past. Still the church had the hurt memory of God's suffering for their sakes. They guarded that title Son of Man with as much jealousy as the Jews had guarded *Yahweh*. To this very day the church in her worship life has refrained from addressing Jesus in her prayers as the "Son of Man." They would use other phrases but not this one. This was not simply a matter of right teaching and doctrine; this was a matter of emotion. Here was an expression of God's sorrow over His own suffering which His justice had demanded as the requirement for winning back His rebellious children to Himself.

CHAPTER VIII

A Few Prophetic Allusions

The New Moses

If David represented the epitome of the kings to the Jewish people, so Moses shared a like esteem as God's prophet without peer. The Book of Deuteronomy eulogizes the great prophet with the tribute that he was the one prophet whom the Lord knew face to face. This affection and devotion to Moses is still found among the Jews even to our day. Devotion to Moses unfortunately cannot be equated with acquaintance with his writings. Most Jews, like most Christians, have become Biblical illiterates. Just as Matthew has portrayed Jesus as the new David, to indicate that He is the ultimate king, so He also holds up Jesus as the new Moses since Jesus reveals God and is Himself the revelation of God on earth.

For the Jews, Moses was *the prophet*. The rest of the prophets were really only interpretative commentaries on the work of the Egyptian-born Jew. Moses so represented the will and voice of God that his name became synonomous for the Scriptures. Quoting Moses as an authority on any issue was to quote God's own authority. Jesus was very much like His Jewish contemporaries in that He frequently clinched an argument with a reference to Moses. In one place He accused the Jews of having a sham belief in the writings of Moses, saying that if they had really believed in Moses they would have believed Him, since Moses had written of Him. Reference to Moses' writing could be made simply by mentioning Moses, as Abraham does in the story of the rich man and Lazarus, "they have Moses and the prophets . . ." or the word Law, the *Torah*, as Jesus does in the Sermon on the Mount, "think not that I am come to destroy the *law* or the prophets." Primarily the Law referred to Moses' writings, but with the passing of time it was applied to the entire Jewish Scriptures.

This does not mean that the Jews believed that Moses had written the entire Old Testament, but it does mean that his ideas are reflected on every page. Rebellion against God meant not taking Moses' writings seriously; and repentance meant returning to God's directives given through Moses' writings; and even the Psalms praise the God who was once revealed through Moses' writings. Psalm 1 speaks about the man who meditates on the Law day and night and takes great delight in doing it. When the writings of Moses and then later his successors are called the Law this does not mean these writings have as their main purpose all kinds of little laws and directions. Law means that these writings are from God Himself and have a permanency which reflects God's absolute nature.

In the Sermon on the Mount Jesus says as long as time goes on not even the most minute alphabetical change will be tolerated. Teaching contrary to it puts the teacher in disfavor with God in the final kingdom. Jesus steps into the world with the twin claims that He is Moses' faithful student and, at the same time, His office is higher than that of any prophet, including Moses.

The Jewish world at the time of Jesus revered Moses very highly, even to the point of legendary exaggeration; but this was not malicious but rather the expression of an overenthusiastic piety. Philo, an Alexandrian Jewish philosopher with strong Greek leanings and also a contemporary of Jesus, called Moses the greatest lawgiver, high priest, and prophet that the world had ever known. His language was so extravagant in his praise for the prophet that Moses actually took on the characteristics of a god. In an apocryphal book, *The Assumption of Moses*, coming from the same general period as Philo, Joshua says that at the occasion of Moses' death no grave was sufficient to hold his body, with the result that his sepulchre had to be as vast as the earth itself. Josephus, the famous Jewish historian, another contemporary, said of Moses that "our lawgiver was a divine man." Also afloat among the Jews was the belief that Moses would appear before the end time. On that account he was placed in the same category with Enoch and Elijah who had never tasted death.

More in line with a saner approach was a belief not in the actual return of Moses, but in the appearance of a prophet like Moses sent by God Himself. This hope was rooted in Deuteronomy 18:15, 18, where Moses promises that after his death there would come another prophet through whom God would speak just as He had done through Moses. In some way the final eschatological deliverance would be patterned after the Exodus delivery out of Egypt which God had accomplished through Moses. Here Jews and Christians have a common heritage and understanding. It would be along these lines that Matthew would present Jesus as the new Moses.

To present all that the New Testament writers say about Jesus and Moses cannot be done here. But at least two references to Jesus' superiority will not interrupt the line of thought. John says in his famous prologue that the Law was given through Moses, but that grace and truth came through Jesus Christ. The writer to the Hebrews says that both Moses and Jesus had supervision over all God's house, but with this difference: Moses exercised this authority as a servant or manager and Jesus as God's own Son.

However, Matthew paints a picture of Jesus as the new Moses which perhaps only the Jew can ever really appreciate; and in a sense this makes it of more value, comparatively speaking. Luke describes the birth of Jesus in nice Christmas language. The story of the inn, the angels, the shepherd, and the adoration are beautiful themes that have rightfully crept into Christian art, including U. S. Postal Service stamps. Matthew's information does not so easily lend itself to merry festive celebration. The first full chapter, at least according to our English Bibles, is the account of how a wicked king plots to kill the infant Child and how in the end the Child escapes with His parents to Egypt for safety. The final deliverance is the return of the Child to Palestine. The Jew who was well acquainted with the story of the birth of Moses in the Book of Exodus could easily see here in the birth of Jesus the birth of another Moses. Herod's order of execution of all the baby boys in Bethlehem resembles the Pharaoh's command to kill all Jewish baby boys in Egypt. They are also alike in that Pharaoh and Herod were both Gentiles, non-Jewish, but still they reign over God's faithful as tyrannical kings. They are both opponents of the true religion. Moses is miraculously saved through the ingenuity of his mother who places him in a boat in Egypt's river. Jesus is also saved by the miraculous intervention of an angel who warns the stepfather to flee with the Child and His mother to Egypt. Moses spends the first years of his life under the direct protection of the Egyptian government, just as Jesus would His. Moses' deliverance out of the Egyptian captivity was to be the established pattern of God's future delivery of His people. Matthew signals the reader to this final delivery in Jesus when he includes the words: "Out of Egypt I have called My Son."

Matthew continues to drop Mosaic footprints when he describes the 40-day sojourn of Jesus in the wilderness. Many streams of thought come together here. Moses had been prepared for the office of prophet by his 40-year exile in the wilderness before God called Him. A more imposing thought is the 40-day sojourn of Moses on Mount Sinai when God dictated to him the laws for the governing of Israel. Exodus specifically says that for 40 days and *nights* Moses conversed with God without eating or drinking. Matthew, Mark, and Luke all describe Jesus' fasting with obvious reference to the first Moses. Only Matthew — and he must want to make the point very clear — includes not only the 40 days, but also the 40 *nights*. At this point Matthew is directing His account specifically to the Jews in the congregations. Some Jews must also have been thinking about how Moses had led their ancestors through the Sinai desert for 40 years before taking them to the Promised Land. The writer to the Hebrews is more explicit on this point, but it is hardly lacking in the Gospels.

Not coincidental is Jesus' giving the Law in the Sermon on the Mount right after the 40-day stay in the wilderness, just as Moses had first given the Law after he had been with God for 40 days and nights. This mountain theme as the place for God's giving a revelation to Moses is not only alluded to by the Sermon on the Mount, but also by the Transfiguration and the final command (or Law) in Matthew 28. In all of these places Jesus appears as Moses. On the Mount of the Transfiguration He appears with Moses, the first lawgiver, and Elijah, the law defender, discussing with them the Law's penalty — death for the sinner. This death Jesus had to face in Jerusalem. Jesus' final command to evangelize the world is also given from a mountain. Like Moses, He concludes His ministry on a mountain. The disciples are bound to all the words of Jesus, as Moses had obligated the Jews. With the command "to teach all nations" the new Moses universalizes the revelation made to the first Moses by making it mandatory for the church to go to the Gentiles. Moses is no longer just the national but in Jesus has become the universal prophet.

The Sermon on the Mount is actually Jesus' interpretation of the Ten Commandments that God had revealed through Moses. Jesus' comments on total loyalty to God, regardless of the difficulties, is a beautiful commentary on the First Commandment to have no other gods. Killing, adultery, swearing, stealing, slandering are among the other topics. Jesus joins Himself to the prophetic line of the Old Testament, since the task of all of the Old Testament prophets after Moses was to apply Mosaic directives in their fullest sense to people who did not comprehend them any more.

Right after the Sermon on the Mount, Jesus establishes His claim as the final Mosaic prophet in Israel with miracles: the centurion's servant is healed, Peter's mother-in-law is healed, the demoniac is exorcised, and Jairus's daughter is restored to life. The miracle perhaps relating Jesus most closely to Moses is the healing of the leper. A sign to Moses that he really was God's prophet came when he placed his hand in his shirt and it came out leprous; when he repeated this action, it came out clean and healthy. Jesus was sure of His prophetic authority, but the healing of the leper identified Him as the new Moses to others.

Not every allusion to Moses can be given, but perhaps a final one showing Moses' redemptive significance for the Jews would be appropriate. Moses was associated with God's redemption of the Jews out of Egypt. The Passover was the blood feast commemorating this occasion, one which the Jews could never forget and which became the basis of all their future hopes. Jesus on the night before the shedding of His blood instituted the Christian Passover which commemorates the blood death of Jesus and which is to be repeated with more frequency than the annual celebration of the Passover; this is a reminder that through the death of God's Lamb, mankind was being released from the captivity of sin through the exodus of the resurrection. The first Moses used the blood of a lamb; the second Moses was Himself the Lamb and used His own blood.

And More Than Moses

There are several places in the Gospel where the Jews recognize Jesus as a prophet. Generally this type of confession is less than what God ultimately demands, still this does not mean that Jesus is not a prophet. One contemporary prominent theologian believes that it is improper to call Jesus a prophet since the typical formula designating a prophet in the Old Testament is lacking in the case of Jesus. This formula, "the word of the Lord came" or a phrase similar to it, indicates a person whom God has chosen as a prophet. This observation is correct. The phrase is never used of Jesus; but Luke, for one, is acquainted with it, as he writes that "the word of God came to John the son of Zechariah."

Jesus is a prophet in the sense that He is God's final spokesman on earth; but in another sense He is not a prophet because when Jesus speaks, He speaks for nobody except Himself. The prophets before Him, including John, all received an *outside* authority from God and spoke for God, not themselves. Jesus as God has *internal* authority and an appeal to a higher authority who sent Him is not necessary, as was the case with the prophets. The Sermon on the Mount indicates the super-prophetic authority of Jesus. There is no introduction about the speaker, His person, authority, or function, but merely the proclamation of One who is God Himself, "Blessed are the poor in spirit . . ." He appears as the ultimate giver of the Law and not only as mediator of the

Law, as Moses, or his interpreters, and as the other prophets were.

In Jesus, God, the Lawgiver, and the prophet, the Law's interpreter, are merged and become one. Before the time of Jesus, God and the prophet are separate. In Jesus they are joined. Previously the word of God must be carried from God to the prophet. Jesus has made this procedure antiquated. As the Law's giver, He knows how it is to be fulfilled. He has the inherent right to change the Law, but renounces this right. A softening of the Law is not permitted. He recites various of the Ten Commandments and after the recitation introduces the absolute interpretation with the words "but I say unto you." Here is God Himself speaking.

The Sermon on the Mount closes with Jesus placing His words on the same level as God's words in the parable of the houses built on sand and rock. Keeping the words of Jesus bestows eternal security. His life is kept safe by God forever. Those who heard Jesus knew that they had more than a prophet on their hands. The crowds are described as being astonished since Jesus taught as Someone who had authority and not like the scribes. The scribes had weighed the value of one passage of the Scripture against another. Jesus taught from His own person. Moses spoke about God; Jesus spoke about Himself.

Let's Not Forget About Jonah: A Prophet to the Gentiles

If Jonah had not made part of the trip to Nineveh by fish, he would have received much more honor from the church than he has — especially in modern times, when there has been a lot of effort to push him out of history and into legend. Let's consider the Gospel evidence in his case before we push him into mythical oblivion. Consider this. The so-called major prophets, Isaiah, Jeremiah, and Daniel are mentioned by name, but none of the so-called minor prophets with the exception of Jonah are mentioned. He is referred to *twice*. To be sure the minor prophets are quoted and alluded to, but not explicitly mentioned by name.

Second, no passage from the Book of Jonah is specifically

quoted, but the prophet himself is held up as example. In other words, there is not so much passage citation from the Book of Jonah, but rather the person of Jonah is held up for comparison with Jesus. Not even the major prophets receive this kind of high treatment.

Third, Jesus uses the example of Jonah in the case of His own resurrection from the dead and the final Judgment — two eschatological events connected with the end of the age. Since Matthew gives such a prominent place to Jonah, no study of Jesus would be complete without at least a few words.

In the first instance, Jesus brands the scribes and Pharisees as an evil and adulterous generation, when they ask of Him a sign to substantiate His divine commission. With almost near mocking, Jesus turns their attention back 700 or 800 years to the sign of the "fish's stomach." What Jesus is talking about is not difficult to determine. Jonah had been given a commission by God to preach to the Ninevites; this he initially renounced by going in the opposite direction. His dislike of Gentiles proved to be a greater factor in his life than the call of God. God does not like to take no for an answer, so a 3-day "ordination" service in the fish's stomach is arranged for Jonah to usher him into the office of prophet to the Gentiles. Needless to say this would make an impression on anybody concerning the seriousness of God's call into His service. Jonah accepts the commission (who wouldn't?), preaches to the Ninevites, and they are converted.

Jesus uses that occasion for a launching pad to describe His own mission. He did not have to be convinced of the office God had given Him, but His enemies did. The ultimate prophetic sign that Jesus provided the Jews (and hence also the whole world) was His resurrection from the dead. Still this does not convince the Jews. At the end of the Gospel there is the account of how they tried to suppress the resurrection evidence even after it had become an accomplished fact.

Jesus here parallels His own ministry to Jonah's by contrast. Jonah is an unwilling prophet. Jesus is willing. Jonah is sent to the Gentiles. Jesus is sent to the Jews. The Gentiles receive the sign of less value: Jonah's sojourn in the fish. The Jews receive the sign of more value: Jesus' stay in the earth followed by the Resurrection. The Gentiles got the poorer preacher, Jonah. The Jews heard God's final prophet ("Behold, a greater than Jonah is here"). With much less to go on, the Gentiles were converted. With knowledge and experience of signs that only God Himself could perform, the Jews remained obstinate. On the Last Day, the scribes and Pharisees, Jesus' own contemporaries, shall confront the Ninevites, Jonah's contemporaries — but not as equals. The Ninevites shall sit in judgment on the unbelieving Jews. (Also participating in this judgment will be the "queen of the south." She believed what God had revealed through Solomon; and how insignificant he is in comparison to Jesus. "Behold, a greater than Solomon is here.") A similar incident occurs in an encounter that Jesus has with the Pharisees and Sadducees. There the conversation is abrupt. When asked for a sign, Jesus merely refers them to Jonah and lets the matter rest at that.

At first it might seem too difficult to determine why Matthew, the Jewish evangelist, gives so much attention to a really minor prophet. In addition, the book with this prophet's name is one of the shortest in the Old Testament. Of course the value of contrasting the ministry of Jonah and Jesus is obviously effective, as was just shown. Still there is another point. The other prophets worked among the Jews, almost exclusively. Naaman the leper makes contact with Elisha, — but on Jewish territory and on the prophet's terms. Even at that the prophet does not speak with him directly but through an intermediary, the scheming Gehazi. Jonah is the really first Gentile prophet we know of, in the fullest sense of the term, regardless of his obvious distaste for the *goyim*, a derisive Hebrew term for Gentiles. God had informed Abraham in the initial promise that he would have a sacramental significance for the world. Those not related to him by blood would eventually share in the same promise. Jonah's mission fits under this category of making Abraham a blessing to the Gentiles. In Jesus the promise would reach fruition.

The Gentile *magi* travel a long distance to pay homage to an infant Jewish king; the Syrophoenician woman is persistent even in the face of divine obstacles; and an officer in the hated Roman occupation troops reaches the epitome of faith – at least in comparison to the Jews whom Jesus knows. Amidst the darkness of Good Friday, another officer, who might have been in charge of the crucifixion detail that day, confesses that the corpse was "the Son of God." All Gentiles! After the resurrection, Jesus broadens the commission of Jonah. Not only are the Ninevites to be included in God's kingdom, but all nations are now eligible for membership in God's exclusive club.

He Preached About Himself

Some have claimed, without too much thinking, that Jesus had a simple message about God as the Father and about all men as brothers. They further assert that Jesus did not preach about Himself. This corruption happened, so it is claimed, at a later period in the church, when Paul and the other apostles acted very much unlike Jesus and began preaching about Jesus and not about God. By just looking at the words of Jesus we can conclude that Jesus did speak specifically and clearly about Himself.

In one section in Matthew there is an amazing Trinitarian section. Jesus is speaking about how it is possible that He, in distinction from all other men, can know so much about God. "All things have been delivered to Me by My Father, and no one knows the Son except the Father, and no one knows the Father except the Son and anyone to whom the Son chooses to reveal Him." The answer is that the Son knows the Father in the same way that the Father knows the Son. All divine knowledge exists perfectly in each. Jesus the Son is preaching not only about the Father but about Himself and His own unique role as the God revealer. As the sole divine teacher Jesus can even choose children and exclude those who are wise in their own deceits. (Could Matthew here be making a subtle reference to believing infants who were receiving Baptism in the early church?) John's Gospel makes this teaching even clearer. In the prologue that evangelist states that no one has seen God at any time with the exception of the "Only-Begotten Son," who has declared God to us.

The parables provide the best examples of Jesus' preaching about Himself. In the parable of the sower, He is the sower. He is the treasure in the field and the pearl of great price. He is the son for whom the king gives a wedding banquet. He is the vineyard owner's son who meets a violent death at the hands of the tenants of the vineyard. He is the king-judge who makes the final pronouncement over the sheep and the goats. He gives the interpretation to His death as a ransom price for sinners. He outlines the final activities of His life: arrest, trial, crucifixion, burial, and resurrection.

In addition to His person, Jesus discusses also His authority. As stated above, He receives it from the Father. When asked by His enemies about the source of His authority, He replies that He will provide an answer as soon as they answer His question about the origin of John's authority. His enemies are now trapped. If they say that it merely comes from man and it is just another human authority, they face the rage of the common people who revered John's authority as heaven-given. Should they admit John's authority came from heaven then they would be forced into asserting that Jesus also had a heaven-given authority, as Jesus stood head and shoulders over John — in spite of the latter's great gift as a prophet ("Of those born of women none is greater than John").

Moses said in the Book of Deuteronomy that the mark of the *true* prophet in contrast to the *false* prophet is whether what he preaches about really happens. The Jews were told simply to disregard a person with prophetic credentials but whose words did not correspond with what was going to happen. God's people were under obligation to test continually the words of the prophets. Jesus cannot be excluded from this test. The words of the angel at the open tomb on Easter morning have an "I told you so" ring about them. *Of course* the words of a true prophet come to pass.

Jesus in His preaching had told the Jews about His heavenly origin and described what He was doing in His ministry among people. Jesus did speak theologically. Most important He spoke about the end time occurrences in His life and the life of the world. Arrest, crucifixion, and resurrection are behind Him now. These events happened just as He described them. The final Judgment of the world will be the keystone establishing the veracity of His prophetic ministry.

Continuing the Prophetic Authority of Jesus

The final scene in the first Gospel shows Jesus as God's ultimate prophet extending His authority beyond the cultural, national, and racial confines of the Jewish people. He announces that all authority has been given to Him in heaven and earth. While this certainly includes the great cosmic power of God or His omnipotence, it primarily means the teaching authority. All the teaching authority that the Old Testament prophets had from Moses to John the Baptist reaches its pinnacle in Jesus. With John the line of the prophets has come to an end.

Jesus must now provide for the teaching of the world, as He had once provided for the teaching of the Israelites through prophets. Now His spokesmen would be the apostles. Before His crucifixion He had provided them with a dry run by testing them out among the Jews; but even then He had hinted that their ultimate work would be with the Gentiles, including their rulers and kings. His *personal* teaching activities were drawing to a close; but He appoints the Twelve as bearers of the prophetic ministry to all nations.

They would teach — not in the same style of Him who was and will always be without peer — and they would proclaim the same message, "teaching them to observe all things whatsoever I have commanded you." Jesus in His teaching had set the boundaries. Nothing less could be taught, as they had to teach "all things whatsoever" — and nothing different, for whoever broke through the accepted boundaries would barely make it into the kingdom, if he made it at all.

Jerusalem: A Symbol of the Final Judgment

In all of the synoptic Gospels the destruction of the city of

Jerusalem is portrayed in such realistic terms and so closely resembling the actual destruction of the city by the Romans in A. D. 70 that many, if not most, New Testament scholars hold the view that these Gospels just had to have been written after the event had actually happened. To the Christian who believes that God is the Lord of history this is no problem. God sees everything as an eternal present and directs everything according to His will, even His will of judgment.

In one of the final discourses in His ministry Jesus speaks about the destruction of the world *and* the destruction of Jerusalem so that these themes are combined into one. For many this has caused some confusion; however, Jesus' prophetic teaching follows that of the Old Testament prophets where the prophet combines a near future event with a far distant event. A good example of this: Nathan's promise to David about Solomon is combined with the promise of the ultimate Messianic deliverer. The prophets who spoke about the destruction of Jerusalem by the Babylonians around the year 600 B. C. saw in these events the final eschatological judgment of God over all sinners.

According to Jesus, the Jews in the city of Jerusalem at His time had not changed much from their ancestors who had occupied that city. It was to this city that God had sent His spokesmen, and almost without fail they had been given an unfavorable reception by the inhabitants. The Jerusalem contemporaries of Jesus were following environmental and hereditary patterns. Now they would face the same fate — destruction of their city.

But as terrible as this destruction was going to be, much worse would be the final Judgment of the world. Relief from the besieged city of Jerusalem could come simply by retreating to the Judean hills. The only drawbacks are for expectant and nursing mothers. No exclusions are made at the final time of the world. International confusion and warfare are matched by signs in the planets and stars. The last act will be the appearing of Jesus — as suddenly and more startling than lightning flashing in a darkened sky.

Jesus felt so strongly about people being prepared for the unexpected that, in addition to the explicit warnings to be prepared, He told several parables as examples. The parables of the faithful and unfaithful servant, the ten virgins, and the three servants all teach preparedness. In addition Jesus compares the final time to the sudden destruction in the days of Noah. The finality and absoluteness of the Judgment is discussed in the parable of the sheep and the goats.

God is always carrying out His judgment in history. One nation rises to destroy another in God's never-ending pattern of judgment against unbelievers. The Christian is not always in a position to give a prophetic interpretation to past or current history, even when he is sorely tempted to do so.

There is one history to which God has given an interpretation. This is the history of the Jews. In the Biblical history, *Jerusalem fell twice,* once before the Babylonians and again before the Romans. Jerusalem with its fallen walls and unfilled expectations is a sign to God's people that the God of grace is still the God of justice and judgment. As Peter says, people mock God because He threatens but does not seem to carry out His threats. The history of the world and especially of the Jews teaches that God's patience can reach limits. The destruction of Jerusalem is a type of the final judgment. The local and limited judgment upon the Jewish race will be replaced by the cosmic and universal judgment upon the Gentiles. Things will be so bad that faith will be a rare commodity.

CHAPTER IX

Resurrection: The Finale

Resurrection as Authentication

Of all the founders of the major religions, Jesus has the unique distinction of having met a violent death and of predicting His continued existence in life after death and His own resurrection. The early church never proclaimed just the crucifixion of Jesus or His resurrection. Both always went together. The crucified Jesus was resurrected, and the resurrected Jesus had been crucified. Isolating either of these two occurrences was to pervert the Christian message to the point of destruction. The resurrection account in all the Gospels appears without embellishment. The matter of fact attitude can be a little unnerving, to say the least. The Gospel writers do not change their tone of voice but continue in their usual writing style. But of course if God is God, what else would you expect?

Those who were brought up with the questions and answers in the Catechism know the question which is answered by telling what Christ's resurrection proves. Don't be offended by the word *prove*. In Jesus God was making a point, and He likes to prove things. The final proof will be the return of Jesus from heaven. The resurrection proves that His teaching is true, that the Father accepted His sacrifice, that He is God, and that all believers will rise to eternal life. Simple as that might sound this agrees with what the Gospel writer is saying.

The resurrection of Jesus puts an exclamation mark behind everything that Jesus is, did, and said. The scribes, the Pharisees, and the Sadducees, and that is a good cross section of the Jewish populace in the first century, all wanted a sign. The sign is the sign of Jonah which prefigures the resurrection of Jesus.

His coming forth from the grave is God's seal of verification to the world. (In the United States official seals do not carry the same weight as they do, for example, in Germany. In that country the seal is revered as authentic proof for most nearly everything. Pardon the exaggeration, but anyone who is personally acquainted with the customs of that country will have a difficult time disagreeing with this assessment.) Three of the things proven: His teaching is true, the Father accepted His sacrifice, and He is God, are really overlapping concepts. After all, He taught that He was God and that the Father would accept the sacrifice. Unless He were God, He could not have offered an acceptable sacrifice. All this has been previously discussed at length. The reader can recheck these things for himself.

The resurrection came as no surprise for Jesus. When He spoke about His death, He always spoke about His resurrection in the same context. The necessity that applied to His death also applied to His resurrection. After all, the Messiah had to die before He entered into His glory. Resurrection is simply the completion of the work of the Messianic servant. Having completed the servant's task, He could put aside the servant's form. He was no longer God in the suffering form of the Son of Man but the glorified Son of God. As Paul says in the introduction to his Letter to the Romans, God had declared Jesus to be the Son of God by the resurrection. To be sure, Jesus was the Son of God before the resurrection, but now He could openly take the name and the honors of this name to Himself. The resurrection is God's sign to the world. Jesus has fulfilled God's purposes, and God has glorified Him.

There is one negative note in the resurrection account. It was alluded to briefly in the discussion of the Virgin Birth and should be repeated here. Within hours of the resurrection, the Jews in Jerusalem were spreading a fabricated account that Jesus' body had been stolen by the disciples. The soldiers were bribed handsomely for their participation in the story. This is not the place to disprove the lack of credibility of this Jewish allegation.

From the beginning the Christian church has had to defend

itself from slanders of this type. All are without historical foundation. The disciples are pictured in the Gospels as scarcely more than cowards, and their carrying out of such a deed would be a false tribute to a courage which they never really had. Since that "third day" to the present, reports are circulated and books are published telling us what "really" happened to the body of Jesus: It was stolen. Jesus was not really dead but walked out of the grave. The grief-stricken disciples thought that Jesus had become alive. Later in the church, some of the leaders *preached* about the resurrection, and thus Jesus became resurrected and alive for the church in *preaching*. These are just a few explanations to avoid what the Gospels teach. Like the witnesses against Jesus at His trial, they don't agree with each other on *what* happened or *how* it happened, but they are certain it did *not* happen as the Gospels describe.

The defense of the resurrection is the church's burden (a delightful one at that!). Jesus talked about His resurrection, and they accused Him of destroying the temple. Paul preached about it, and they laughed and gave him strange stares. We can expect the same treatment. Didn't Jesus say that the disciple is not above his master? Anything less than affirming the resurrection of the body of Jesus (and this certainly includes revivification) is less than Christian.

Resurrection as Final Coronation

Among the pagan peoples who lived alongside the Israelites, there was the custom of an annual coronation day for their king, at the beginning of the New Year festival. There is no record in the Old Testament that any of the Jewish kings during the period of the kingdom engaged in such a practice. This is not to doubt that some of the kings, especially of the Northern Kingdom, Israel, might have introduced this custom into the worship life of the palace or of the royal family. The kings of both Judah and Israel engaged in far worse abominations than this. Still there is no command or prescribed ritual for an annual coronation of a Jewish king.

There are some Old Testament scholars who see the words

in Psalm 2:7, "You are My Son, today I have begotten You" as being taken over or borrowed from the coronation ritual of a king. No one can deny the interesting possibilities of the origin of these words. Nevertheless it is always hazardous to state dogmatically who said what first. Regardless of the origin of these words, they are applied by David to the Messianic king, a king for whom David looked, perhaps in his own time. David died knowing that somehow in Solomon these words, "You are My Son, today I have begotten You" would be directed to their ultimate destination.

Though there is no record of any annual coronation celebration of the Jewish kings, there are in the case of David, at least, three coronation-like occasions. First, David is anointed with oil by Samuel in Bethlehem. This happened as a child and inaugurated him into his first taste of political and military life. Second, David is recognized as the Israelite king by the tribe of Judah at Hebron. Still a third time David is made king. This time is 7½ years after all the tribes of the Israelites gathered at Hebron and proclaimed him king. From this last episode we do have the words of a coronation liturgy. The people said together: "The Lord said to you, 'You shall be shepherd of my people Israel, and you shall be prince over Israel.' " Though these words were probably first spoken to David, they reach their culmination in Jesus who is the Good Shepherd and the Prince of Peace.

The three coronations in the reign of King David set a pattern for Jesus' own acclamation as King. According to the New Testament writers, the words of coronation, "You are My Son, today I have begotten You" apply to Jesus on at least *three* different occasions. It was almost as if Jesus, like His father David, had to be ushered into the office of the king three times. First, at the baptism of Jesus we hear the words of the Father from heaven, "This is My beloved Son." Again at the transfiguration of Jesus the words come from heaven, "This is My beloved Son." Still the royal psalm reaches for fulfillment in the resurrection as Paul claims in his sermon in the synagogue at Antioch of Pisidia.

The words of Psalm 2 as applied to Jesus in the New Testament indicate that He is initiated into the royal office three times: His baptism, His transfiguration, and His resurrection. His baptism set Him in the direction of the royal or Messianic task, very much like David as a boy was confronted with the office of king, when he was chosen by Samuel. At both times there was hardly any public recognition of the royal office of either, with perhaps the exception of those who conducted the rite (Samuel in the case of David and John the Baptist in the case of Jesus).

At Jesus' transfiguration, He has already been recognized as Christ, the Son of God, by His own disciples. This was at least a partial recognition on the part of others. In the same way, David at Hebron received partial recognition as king when the tribe of Judah swore to him their allegiance. Both Jesus and David had started their respective royal activities, but had not brought them yet to a totally satisfactory conclusion.

In the case of David the final and third coronation was connected with the capture of Jerusalem. Jesus' coronation would also come with a conflict in Jerusalem. Just as David's victorious capture of Jerusalem provided the occasion for his acclamation as king by *all* the tribes of Israel, so Jesus by His victorious death in Jerusalem is crowned universal King by His Father in Jerusalem.

The words, "You are My Son, today I have begotten You" began as a trickle when first spoken by David concerning the Messianic king. At the baptism of Jesus, they are spoken louder and at the transfiguration, still even louder. Though no ear heard it, they cracked heaven's vaulted chambers at the resurrection. The true son of God was that Son who did everything that God wanted Him to. David tried! The Lord knows how hard he tried, but human frailties prevented him. Solomon — well, most of the time he didn't even try to be God's son, and he set a pattern for almost all of his successors.

In Jesus, God's true Son does all that God expects. The resurrection is the public proclamation that Jesus is entitled to be both King and Son. (Let the reader understand this correctly. Of course, Jesus is God's Son from eternity and King over all as Creator.) The resurrection does not mean that God is now taking off the masquerade. Rather it means that as man and more particularly David's Son He has *earned* the right to be God's King and Son.

The Forty Days

According to the record supplied by Luke, Jesus was on earth for 40 days between His resurrection and His ascension into heaven. On the surface all the Gospel writers are a little disappointing on what they report — at least in regard to the quantity of the material. Matthew, who has been our primary guide up to this point, reports only the few words of Jesus to Mary instructing the disciples to get to Galilee and the commission to make disciples out of all nations. Mark, if we accept the shortest ending and there is no cogent reason not to, reports no actual words of Jesus at all. Luke and John fill in the most details, but this is hardly more than tying up the loose ends. John might have originally ended his Gospel with what we know today as chapter 20. The last verse in chapter 20, about this Gospel being written to bring people to faith in Jesus as the Son of God, makes a perfectly good ending to any Gospel! Perhaps on some other occasion he penned what we know as chapter 21. The endings of both of these chapters with their little homilies on the value of the written Word certainly are parallel. Veteran preachers frequently come to the end of their sermons more than once!

Taking all four Gospels together we note something common to all of them: Jesus has already ended His teaching ministry in the sense of teaching them anything new. The period of teaching ended with the crucifixion. They had already been instructed in Christian doctrine, though their comprehension of it had been a little less than desired. Jesus is no longer performing the same type of miracles as authenticating signs of the reliability of His teaching. This is in no way to deny the miraculous nature of Jesus' visiting the disciples behind locked doors, as Luke reports, or the catch of 153 fish, as John reports. But this is to assert that in the light of the resurrection, a miracle which is simply without equal, all other miracles are not only unnecessary but would be a letdown. It's the old business of holding a candle in the face of the, sun. In comparison to the resurrection, anything else would be a disappointment. Besides, in the resurrection of Jesus God had made His point. Of all the events, this needed the least interpretation.

Jesus' appearances over the 40 days were for the benefit of the disciples (here the wider sense is intended) and not for Jesus. The resurrection had meant that He already shed all marks of His humility; but He did not shed Himself of His body. Already at the time of His resurrection Jesus had gone to the Father in glory. The ascension was His public departure from the disciples. During those 40 days, He "stepped out of the Father's glory." Jesus was hardly waiting around! This was not the Son of Man looking for a place to sleep. Paul says in the salutation to the Roman Christians: by the resurrection the Father declared Jesus to be the Son of God.

The 40 days were for the psychological benefit of the disciples to give them a chance to pull themselves together after what had been the world's most shattering experience – the return to life of a man who had been publicly executed. Jesus, though now glorified, is now stooping low to the earth again to help man. Where the Gospels picture the disciples, they picture them as men who have undergone a deep psychological shock. Though they are normal, rational men, they have experienced something which their normal experiences up to that time could not really handle – not even in an inadequate way.

At the first report from the women about the empty tomb, some, like Peter and John, go to see for themselves. John waits outside! Amazing! One wonders with what thoughts his mind was haunted. Two "sub-disciples" return to Emmaus, where they apparently lived. These were hardly men so totally in charge of their emotions that they were capable of making a decision of totally abandoning what Jesus had taught. Before the sun sets on that first Easter Day, the ten disciples' thoughts have turned away from the theological questions of the resurrection to the political questions of Roman and Jewish repression.

Even later when the disciples resume their occupation as fishermen in Galilee, they still have not put the pieces of the puzzle together. Let not their action be interpreted to mean that they considered the tasks given them by Jesus as unimportant. They simply did not know how to handle a new situation in which Someone had come back from the dead.

Perhaps the closest thing that we experience still today would be the news of a sudden death in the family. Psychologists tell us that for a short period of time we go into a shock in which we even cut off the tragic reality. The shock of the resurrection must have been one of even greater proportions. Life is a preparation for death. Death is an everyday reality and never comes on us totally without any warning. Resurrection is an entirely new action of God in the world's history. The disciples were totally human and reacted just like people in shock react. If they had reacted rationally, then we might have become a little suspicious. It was a shock that would take more than a few days to recover from.

During this period of shock and recovery Jesus is no Olympian god scaring people half out of their wits with the miracle to end all miracles. He is the picture of patience. During this period of emotional crises, He is the Good Shepherd who still cares for His own and is the Father who quietly waits for the prodigal sons. In Matthew and Mark there are simple instructions to go to Galilee. Those poor disciples were probably not capable of comprehending much more at that moment. Even in ordinary moments they are called men of little faith. In Luke-Acts there are three episodes, each very similar to the other. To the Emmaus disciples there is the simple repetition of Jesus' teachings on the framework of the Old Testament. That night there is the appearance of Jesus to the disciples in Jerusalem with the quiet assurance that He is risen from the dead and that the first order of business is their own internal peace and serenity.

Just before the ascension, the disciples pose what seems like a silly question about the political restoration of Israel to past glories. (You would think that by now they would have buried their foolish millenialism.) Jesus does not rebuke them, but simply urges them to wait for the fuller understanding of His words which the Holy Spirit would supply.

The Gospel of John is very similar to Luke's in picturing Jesus with infinite patience. After He soothes the disciples with His own personal presence, He even gets down to the same level as Thomas and invites him to put his fingers into the very parts of Jesus' body designated by Thomas — a condition for belief so far as Thomas was concerned.

John also has the incident of the restoration of Peter to his office on the shore of Lake of Galilee. For some time Peter must have been pulling his hair out in anticipation of what Jesus would say to him. He, the chief disciple, had let Jesus down in the very moments when he had promised fidelity. Not being blessed with the gift of sitting down, he suggested fishing. Their boats still waited for them up in the north country. What better way was there to forget about their troubles? Spotting Jesus on the shore, he dives into the water with the same impulsive spirit for which he would later become famous. This in spite of the fact that it seems that some of his colleagues, at least John, were in better physical shape than he was. Peter's emotions were torn between his own sense of failure and an undying sense of ambition. He probably expected immediate forgiveness and restoration. Well, he received it but not so immediately. His greatness in the church would involve children as well as congregational leadership and in the end his greatness would be sealed with a martyr's death. Jesus did not destroy that ambition — He merely directed it along other lines.

Those 40 days really get their importance from what Jesus was going to do. By the end of the period, they had accepted the fact of the resurrection, but they did not know how to fit it into the general scheme of God's great plan. Jesus had to ascend into heaven for *their* benefit, not for *His*. Had He stayed much longer, a cult might have developed around Him. Jesus came not so much to be worshiped by His followers. He had come to seek and to save the lost. Jesus could have had all the angels in heaven if personal attention were His highest goal. The disciples were not so much to be worshippers of Jesus but witnesses of the salvation that He had accomplished by the cross and empty tomb. First there were the Jews, then the Samaritans, and then finally the entire world.

A mammoth task for men whose abilities were not always the best! They are not permitted to gaze into heaven, but they are to travel to the earth's four corners and to search into every corner on the way. Hardly a new task for them, as Jesus had commissioned them at the beginning of His ministry to become "fishers of men."

In all four Gospels there are the promises of the Holy Spirit. Jesus had carried out His work by the power of the Spirit, and those who were led to accept Him as God's final Messiah also did so by the Spirit. God never works without His Spirit! The Spirit whom Jesus promised would be the Spirit who would teach them, lead them, and speak through them. There would be no new doctrinal facts. Jesus had already done this. He was *the* Teacher. No further instruction is needed. Rather the Spirit would work on their minds so that they could see the teachings of Jesus in the right relationship. After all their problem was not facts, but putting them in the right order. It's the distinction between knowledge and wisdom. They had been called by Jesus not for their own glory but for what they could do for Him in explaining to the world His sacrifice. That question about restoring the kingdom to Israel at that time was such a selfish question.

Little did they know at that time that through their preaching *they* would bring in a kingdom that would be greater in respect to area, numbers, and years than any kingdom that David, Solomon, or any Caesar would or could ever bring. The story of their work engendered by the Holy Spirit must be left for another volume. Wherever you hear someone calling Jesus "Lord," there the Spirit is spreading the Father's kingdom through the words of men who had wanted personal greatness but who instead became great for God.

Ascension and Presence

Matthew, like Mark and John, does not conclude with Christ's ascension. The best account that we have of it is not in the Gospels, but in the Acts of the Apostles. The first Gospel merely closes with the words, "Lo, I am with you to the end of the age." In excluding the ascension, perhaps Matthew, and with him

Mark and John, are teaching a truth of equal value that Jesus continues His presence with the church even though He cannot be seen by the human eye. The presence is intimately connected with His name or His Word. It can be found where people are teaching everything He taught. This is the mark of the true disciples — abiding in Jesus' Word. Jesus can be found in these same words to this very day. You will not find Him in the sword of Peter and the political machinations of men. He is not found in fantastic works and miracles. This is the glory of preaching, which conforms to His Word. It is the home of Jesus in this world.